The R Rules

A guide for teens to identify and build resources

The R Rules

A guide for teens to identify and build resources

Elizabeth W. Souther

Contributing author: Ruby K. Payne, Ph.D.

The R Rules: A guide for teens to identify and build resources © 2008 by aha! Process, Inc.
  Elizabeth W. Souther
  Contributing author: Ruby K. Payne
    175 pp.
    Bibliography pp. 157–161

aha! Process, Inc.
P.O. Box 727
Highlands, TX 77562-0727
(800) 424-9484 or (281) 426-5300
Fax: (281) 426-5600
Website: http://www.ahaprocess.com

Edited by Jesse Conrad
Book design by Betti Souther
Illustrations by Suzanne Howard
Cover design by ArtLink

        ISBN 13: 978-1-934583-10-4
        ISBN 10: 1-934583-10-3

1. Title

Table of Contents

INTRODUCTION

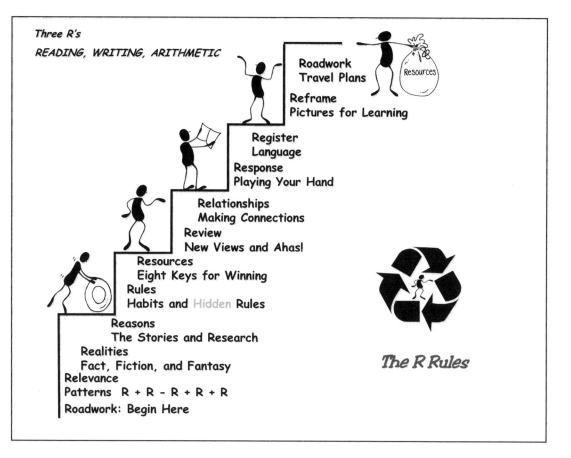

Three R's
READING, WRITING, ARITHMETIC

Roadwork
Travel Plans

Reframe
Pictures for Learning

Register
Language

Response
Playing Your Hand

Relationships
Making Connections

Review
New Views and Ahas!

Resources
Eight Keys for Winning

Rules
Habits and Hidden Rules

Reasons
The Stories and Research

Realities
Fact, Fiction, and Fantasy

Relevance
Patterns R + R - R + R + R

Roadwork: Begin Here

The R Rules

The R Rules Rules + Rigor + Relationships = Resources + Results + Respect
Rules + Regulations – Relationships = Resentment + Refusal

Three R's—reading, writing, and arithmetic—are very important and necessary, but there are other R's are that are just as important for success in today's complex world. Understanding other R's like realities, resources, "hidden rules," patterns of economic class, and relationships and how they influence the way we think, act, and learn is also vital.

The R Rules is designed to present possibilities and options. Participants will consider information, use tools, and learn processes and strategies to identify and increase resources. When people think of resources they generally think only of financial resources, but other resources like support systems, physical and mental resources, role models, and people who can help and listen are equally important. Participants will ask what, why, and how: What is this information, how it is important to me, and how can it be used to benefit and make a difference in my life and my community?

Life is like a game; you get good hands, and you get bad hands. Knowing the rules of the game, how to use the resources that are available, and how to read the patterns can help you be in control, keep from being cheated, and win more often.

Welcome to *The R Rules*

$$R + R - R = R + R$$

$$R + R + R = R + R + R$$

The R Rules

The R Rules

Culture: The values, beliefs, behaviors, and material objects that together form a people's way of life.

–John J. Macionis

Life is like a card game.

Everyone gets a set of cards.
While you can't control the cards you get ...
You can decide how to play them.

Check the cards in your hand:
> Sometimes the cards in your hand are the same cards that other players were dealt.
> Sometimes they are different.

We all ...
> come from a particular region or part of a country.
> face the possibility of illness or disability.
> have a heritage and are members of a group based on race.
> have intelligence and a formal or informal education.
> will experience the changes of aging as/if we grow older.
> deal with issues and expectations related to gender.
> have an economic reality and belong to an economic class.
> use the rules and patterns we know. *The R Rules* is based on patterns.
> have hopes, fears, and dreams.
> have resources. The amount and how they are used vary depending on the individual.
> face unique challenges.
> use the resources available to meet those challenges.
> are problem solvers.

The R Rules Formulas

Grant East said, "Rules without relationships breed rebellion." R - R = R
R Rules: R + R - R = R + R *or* Rules + Regulations - Relationships = Rebellion + Resentment
R + R + R =R + R + R *or* Rules + Rigor + Relationships = Resources + Results + Respect
Rules and rigor with relationships build resources and get results and respect.
"No significant learning occurs without a significant relationship."

–Dr. James Comer

Relationships can be a driver.
They can also be a barrier.
Check your cards for relationships.

      +   Δ

A Future Picture:
What do you want to do, be, or have?
Do and *be* are now ...

Two things that help individuals move
from one economic class to another are
education and relationships.

Individuals often must change how they
spend time in order to move from one
level of achievement to another.

Why?

Another R word:

Resiliency: The ability to succeed and adapt in situations; the ability to recover and develop social competence regardless of exposure to extreme stress.

Rigor

Rules

_____

_____

Relationships

_____

_____

_____

_____

_____

_____

_____

_____

_____

_____

_____

_____

_____

_____

Resources

_____

_____

_____

_____

_____

Respect

_____

_____

_____

_____

Results

_____

_____

_____

_____

_____

For each category, list examples or descriptors of what these look like in your life.

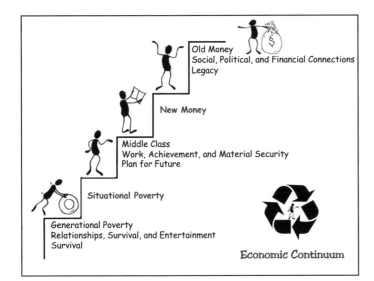

Old Money
Social, Political, and Financial Connections
Legacy

New Money

Middle Class
Work, Achievement, and Material Security
Plan for Future

Situational Poverty

Generational Poverty
Relationships, Survival, and Entertainment
Survival

Economic Continuum

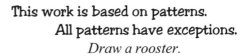

This work is based on patterns.
All patterns have exceptions.
Draw a rooster.

More patterns

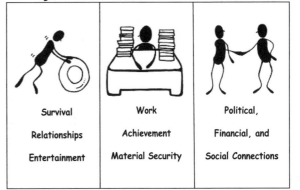

Survival	Work	Political,
Relationships	Achievement	Financial, and
Entertainment	Material Security	Social Connections

Understanding and knowing when to use
"hidden rules" is one resource.
Here are some others:

Resources

Financial
Physical
Emotional
Mental
Spiritual
Support Systems
Relationships and Role Models
Knowledge of Hidden Rules
Mental Models
Language

Choices are based on resources.
When more resources are available,
more choices are available.
Resources = Choices

Poverty: the extent to which an individual
does without resources.
Under-resourced: lacking resources to address a
particular situation or negotiate a particular
environment.
Child: an individual 18 years of age or younger.
Generational: patterns after two generations or longer.
Situational: due to a situation or circumstance.

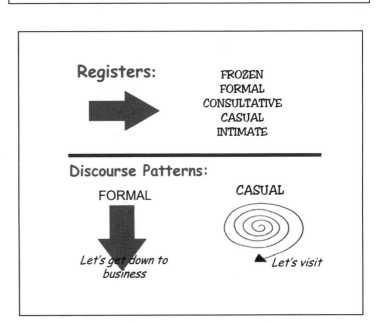

Registers:
FROZEN
FORMAL
CONSULTATIVE
CASUAL
INTIMATE

Discourse Patterns:

FORMAL

Let's get down to business

CASUAL

Let's visit

The R Rules

The R Rules is about patterns and relationships,
about the what, why, and how of
rules, realities, and resources.
I hope *The R Rules* helps you learn about yourself,
about who you are, and who you want to be.
I hope you are inspired to keep learning,
to operate from a place of hope
rather than a place of resignation.
I hope you will see possibilities where you once accepted limits.
I hope you will ask why, and then why not.
I hope you will share what you learn with others
so they too will have choices.
I hope you will not play small,
that you will develop and
show your unique talents and skills,
and by doing so
give others permission to do the same.
I hope you will use your mind as a tool
to invent and discover.
I hope you will use your mind as a weapon
to fight fear and injustice.
I hope you will use your mind as a resource to create
the future you and I want to live in.
I hope you will know the excitement and promise
that only a person beginning a long journey
whose final destination is seen
yet uncertain can know.
I hope you will have courage to take new roads,
I hope you will follow your dreams.
I hope.

Betti Souther

Notes

Chapter 1
ROADWORK

"Begin with the end in mind."
-Stephen Covey

What this is: Roadwork is a term to describe the planning and preparation done before a trip or journey. Roadwork requires making a plan that includes the actions necessary to reach a destination or future picture. Steps like *where* you want to go, *when* you will start and stop, *how long will it take*—with checkpoints along the way—and *how* resources will be used. Life is like a journey. It is important to know where you are going and to have a mental picture of the destination or what you want the future to look like. Stephen Covey says, "All physical creation must first be preceded by mental creation." Everything starts with an idea, a mental picture, or a dream.

In a perfect world people decide what they want to do, be, or have. They make a plan, work hard, and achieve all of the things they set out to do. Unfortunately, real life doesn't always work out that way. Things and people change; plans don't always end up as we pictured them. Opportunities and challenges occur, and future pictures must be reframed or redrawn. Resources and strategies are needed. Having a vision of what you want, goals, and a written plan will help you stay on the right course. A mental picture can help you stay focused on the future even when things don't go exactly as you thought they would, you make a wrong turn, or are forced to take a detour.

Why this is important: In *Alice's Adventures in Wonderland,* Alice asked the Cheshire Cat which way she ought to walk. "That depends a good deal on where you want to get to," said the Cat. When Alice confessed that she didn't much care where she went, the Cat replied, "'Then it doesn't matter which way you go." Knowing where you want to go allows you to plan the work and work the plan. Connecting resources and efforts to a future picture is a way to sort information, see options, and make choices.

How you can use this information: Your mind is a tool, a weapon, and a resource. Create a mental picture of the future you want to live in—a future picture. Use information, strategies, and tools to see patterns, manage time, and decide what is important and what is not. Check your progress, work and rework your plan. Develop resources, skills, and strategies that can be used when the rules or the resources change. Develop self-talk and relationships that encourage and inspire.

What: information for planning, seeing patterns, using resources, playing the game, and making a difference.
Why: Because life is like a game—you get good hands, you get bad hands.
How: You've got to know how to hold 'em, know when to fold 'em, know when to walk away, and when the game is done.

Patterns of this course

Time: days, start and end, progress reports

Space: location, room, assigned seats

Formal Register: course description, state standards, academic vocabulary, school and class rules, vision, mission, and goals

Decoding: course requirements, rubrics, attendance, grading scale, prioritizing, patterns, and processes

Part to Whole: course overview, assignments, resources, student data folders, conferences, weekly class meetings for planning and revision

Where do you want to go?
What do you want to do, be, or have?
What is important to you?

Create a mental picture of the destination.
Set goals to reach it.
    short-term and *long-term*
Write them down and make an action plan:
    Unless you write them and make a plan,
    they are just dreams or hallucinations.
    Consider resources when you plan.
Check your progress:
    One mile at a time,
    use the plan as a map,
    read the signs along the way,
    check how far you have traveled
    and the wear on your vehicle,
    know which direction you are going,
    and the desired destination.
Celebrate accomplishments along the way.
    Ask for directions and change your plans if you
    take a wrong turn or detour.

Create a mental picture.
   Set the goal.
      Plan backward.

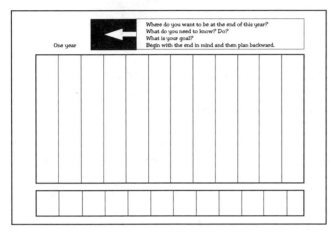

Planning Backward

For a Day, a Week, a Month, a Year

Kickoff

15%

Goal

Percentage of
job completed | 10 | 20 | 30 | 40 | 50 | 60 | 70 | 80 | 90 | 100

Think of the football field: Start working for the goal at one end,
finish when you cross the goal line at the other end.

Why are we here? To do what?

fun think study

Why

How will we make it happen?
Work Study Listen Talk Fun

What do we need to do well together?

What

helping each other

Helping Respecting

Writing a Mission Statement

How

Affinity Diagram
located in Tools
section

Why are we here? To do what?
What do we need to do well together?
How will we make this happen?

As a learning community:

Who are we? What is our purpose? Why does this class/group exist?
If we were the best we could be, what would that look like ...
   by the end of this grading period?
   by the end of this year?
What collective commitments are we willing to make to be the best?
What do we agree to do together to reach our goals?
What beliefs are we willing to turn into behaviors?
What intentions are we willing to turn into results?
What targets and timelines are we willing to set and use to measure progress?
How will we measure success?
What resources are available to help us reach our goals?

Learning communities build on a foundation of:
- Shared vision: a future picture
- Mission or purpose: what, why, and how
- Guiding principles: rules and commitments
- Goals: steps to make it happen
- Working in teams
- Collaborating and building resources

Focus on:
- Inquiry and exploration
- Sorting data and information
- Using results to see patterns
- Continuing to find a better way

Building TEAMS

Identify *Who:* Consider resources and what needs to be done. Identify
   roles: leader, facilitator, members, timekeeper, recorder.
Identify *What:* What will be accomplished? State it in common
   language as a goal. Set short-term and long-term goals. Create
   a rubric or measure for evaluation of the finished product.
Identify *How:* Use a Planning Backwards tool and action plan. Translate
   the goal into steps using step charts, timelines, and tools.
   Agree on team rules and behaviors, discuss processes,
   procedures, and progress indicators. Write a timetable that
   includes a start, finish, and when to check progress. Plan time
   for teacher assistance and direction.

Adapted from the work of Eaker, DuFour, and DuFour

Monday	Tuesday	Wednesday	Thursday	Friday

Grade: *80/20 Rule*

				%					%
				%					%
				%					%
				%					%
				%					%

Attendance Goal:

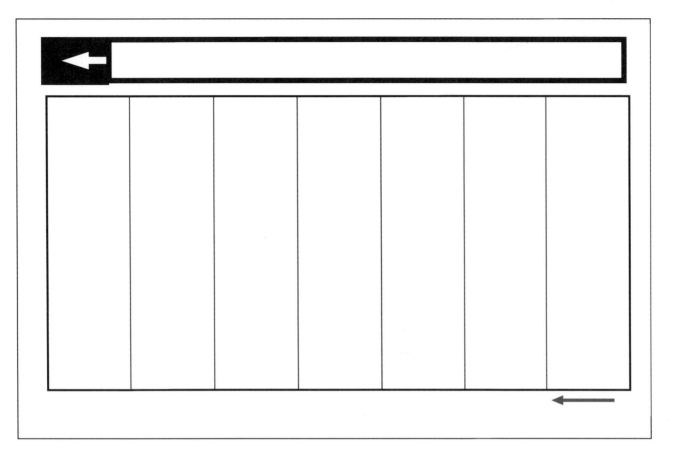

Monday	Tuesday	Wednesday	Thursday	Friday	Saturday	Sunday
1. 2. 3. 4. 5.	1. 2. 3. 4. 5.	1. 2. 3. 4. 5.	1. 2. 3. 4. 5.	1. 2. 3. 4. 5.	1. 2. 3. 4. 5.	1. 2. 3. 4. 5.

Keep	Start	Stop

Create a mental picture.

1. What are you trying to do, be, or have?
2. Who will be involved?
3. Why are you doing this? What will be accomplished?
4. How will you do this? Strategy, Action Plan, Steps, Times
5. What resources are needed? Available?
6. How will you measure results, know you've reached your goal?
7. When will you start? How long will it take to do this?
   When and how often will you check your progress?
   When do you expect to finish the work?

Set a goal

Write SMART Goals and Action Plans

SMART Goal and Action Plan
September 6th:
    I will get an A in English on my October 20th report card by doing and turning in all my assignments and homework, participating in class, and studying for the test.
    I will write down my grades every day. Every Friday during 6th hour I will total and average them. If necessary, I will ask for extra work to improve my grade.

Support: Mrs. James before school, tutor after school.

Is this a
- S   Specific
- M   Measurable
- A   Action
- R   Result/Resources
- T   Timeline

goal?

SMART GOALS

The parts of a goal are:
what, who, why, how, and when

SMART Goals are:
Specific, can be Measured, have an Action plan, Results, and a Timeline.

Specific	Measurement	Actions	Results	Timeline
Who will do what? **What** is the goal or desired outcome?	**Measure** Why are you doing this? What specifically will be improved or accomplished?	**How** List a strategy. Develop an action plan with steps.	**Consider** Future picture Realistic Relevant Resources	**When** will the goal be accomplished? Completion date

Plan your work, work your plan.
The steps used to accomplish a goal are called an
ACTION PLAN.

SMART ACTION PLAN

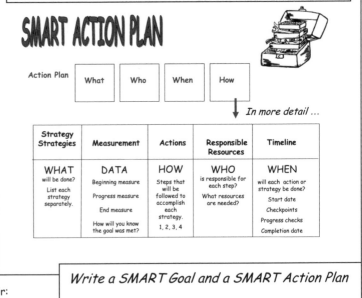

Action Plan | What | Who | When | How |

In more detail ...

Strategy Strategies	Measurement	Actions	Responsible Resources	Timeline
WHAT will be done? List each strategy separately.	**DATA** Beginning measure Progress measure End measure How will you know the goal was met?	**HOW** Steps that will be followed to accomplish each strategy. 1, 2, 3, 4	**WHO** is responsible for each step? What resources are needed?	**WHEN** will each action or strategy be done? Start date Checkpoints Progress checks Completion date

Action Plan:

What	Why	How

What will I do first?   How much time will be needed for this task?

1.
2.
3.
4.
5.
6.
7.
8.
9.
10.

What resources are needed?
Why are they needed?
How will I use them?
Who will I talk to if I need help?

Goals without action plans are like sitting in a rocking chair:
You feel good, but you don't get anywhere.

Write a SMART Goal and a SMART Action Plan

What do you want to do?
Why do you want to do this?
How will you do this?

How do you plan to go to college? By car.

A Goal:

1. What do you want to do, be, or have? Why? How can you accomplish this? Consider several options.
2. If your future was the best it could possibly be, what would it look or be like?
  Consider places, people, things, accomplishments, and activities.
  Create a picture in your mind. This is your future picture—a mental model.
3. Write a SMART Goal: *Specific*, includes *Measures, Action* or strategy, desired *Results*, and *Timeline*.
4. Check the goal to make sure it is realistic and relevant for what you want to accomplish. For example, changing a grade
  in math class from an F to an A in one day may not be realistic.
5. Check the three R's: realistic, relevant, resources.
6. Use a Planning Backwards tool to see the steps needed to use the strategy listed in your goal.
7. Write a SMART action plan.

An Action Plan:

1. Strategies: Refer to your goal and list all of the strategies that will be used to accomplish the goal. Consider strategies
  such as studying more, a mentor, tutor, etc. depending on the goal.
2. Measurement: Write the start measurement; for example, "I have an F in Math. " List the end measurement you are
  trying to reach with this goal, for example having an A in Math.
3. Actions: For each strategy list the steps that will be taken to reach your goal. First, then, etc.
4. Responsible: List who will be responsible for the actions in each step. When listing people who will be assisting or
  responsible for helping you reach your goal, check with them to make sure they are willing and can work within the
  timelines stated in the plan.
5. Resources: List what resources are needed for each step. Consider options or different resources that could be used if
  resources you want are not available. Include self-talk, mental models, and role models.
6. Realistic: Reality check. Think big enough to see possibilities and small enough to check realities.
7. Timeline: Write down the date work will start. Write down the date work will be completed. List dates for
  each step. Schedule regular dates to check your progress toward reaching the goal.
8. Check self-talk, the stories you tell yourself. Reframe information, resources, and options when necessary.
9. Have courage to try and stamina to keep going. If things are not working, consider options and other resources
  and revise your plan. Things may not go exactly the way you thought they would. You may not be able to
  control the hand you are dealt; however, you can read the patterns, get rid of cards that are not helping you win,
  draw new cards, and decide how you play the game.

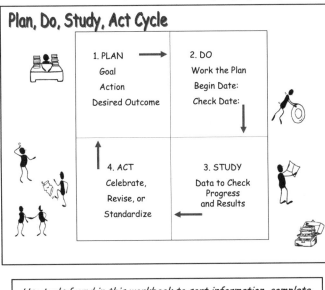

Use tools found in this workbook to sort information, complete
tasks, increase resources, and use patterns.

Einstein said:
"It is not that I am so much smarter
than other people, I am just willing
to stay with a problem longer than most."

Dreams are travels for the soul.
Where do you travel?
Where do you want to go?

If my dream came true,
it would it look like ...

Weekly Student Planner

Name: _____ Class: _____ Hour: 1 2 3 4 5 6 7 8 Time: _____ Location: _____ Teacher: _____

Week of	Monday	Tuesday	Wednesday	Thursday	Friday
Assignments					
Learning Goals					
Academic Vocabulary					
Resource Check					
Skill Building					
Assignment complete? Y/N					
Journal entry complete? Y/N					
Attendance? + - On Time? Y/N					
My work ethic was + / -					
My attitude was + / -					
Daily Grade/Average Grade					
Content Grade/Process Grade					
My GOAL FOR THIS WEEK is					

Action Plan: _____

GOAL FOR NEXT WEEK: _____

Action Plan: _____

Monday	Tuesday	Wednesday	Thursday	Friday	Saturday	Sunday

Monday	Tuesday	Wednesday	Thursday	Friday	Saturday	Sunday

Codes for Skills: N = Note Taking   DS = Data Systematically   T = Time Management   CE = Cause/Effect   S = Summarizing   G = Goal Setting   W = Writing
CC = Compare /contrast   SQ = Sequencing   TS = Task Time and Steps   V = Voice   R= Formal Register   O= Other

Adapted from the work of Susan Kannard

Progress Check Sheets

Check progress in each class. Ask the teacher to fill out one square and use the information to see patterns, make improvements, and develop resources.

Name:

Date:

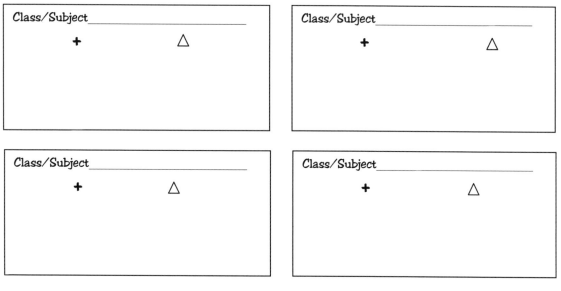

Class/Subject_____	Class/Subject_____
+ △	+ △

Class/Subject_____	Class/Subject_____
+ △	+ △

Notes:

- -

Name: Date:

Class:_____ Current Grade_____
    Drivers   Barriers

Class:_____ Current Grade_____
    Drivers   Barriers

Class:_____ Current Grade_____
    Drivers   Barriers

Class:_____ Current Grade_____
    Drivers   Barriers

Notes:

SMART GOALS

The parts of a goal are:
what, who, why, how, and when

SMART Goals are:
Specific, can be *Measured*, and have an *Action, Results,* and a *Timeline.*

Specific	Measurement	Actions	Results	Timeline
Who will do what?	**Measure**	**How**	**Consider**	**When**
What is the goal or desired outcome?	Why are you doing this? What specifically will be improved or accomplished?	List a strategy. Develop an action plan with steps.	Future Picture Realistic Relevant Resources	Goal will be accomplished or End time

Who will do *what,* by *when,* and *how?*

Date:_____

_____will_____

_____

by_____. I will know my goal has been reached when_____

_____. In order to

accomplish this I will_____

_____

_____

_____.

I will check progress toward this goal on_____.

Resources available:

Notes

Chapter 2
RELEVANCE

Life is like a card game ...
you get good hands,
you get bad hands.

The R's

Roadwork: *goal setting, planning tools, and action plans*
Relevance: *what, why, and how of* The R Rules
Realities: *facts, perceptions, data, and key points*
Reasons: *the stories we tell ourselves, research, and 'root causes'*
Rules: *unwritten cues, behaviors, and three sets of hidden rules*
Resources: *eight key resources for success and living well*
Review: *mindsets, habits, paradigms, and roles*
Relationships: *understanding connections, purpose, and patterns*
Response: *using resources related to a future picture*
Register: *language, words, and their power*
Reframe: *translating concrete and abstract*
Roadwork: *planning and preparing for where you want to go*

R Rules *Mental Model or Pattern:*

Rules + Rigor + Relationships =
Resources + Results + Respect

The first R formula:

$$R + R - R = R + R$$ -Grant East

Regulations – Relationship =
Resistance + Rebellion

Based on the work of Dr. Ruby Payne, we will:
- Draw a picture of your future and make a plan to get there.
- Use strategies and tools to set goals and measure progress.
- Identify patterns, realities, and resources.
- Explore economic classes, hidden rules, cultures, and habits.
- Identify and discuss realities, paradigms, and mental models.
- Analyze eight resources and complete a personal resource inventory.
- Discuss and identify relationships, roles, and role models.
- Reframe responses, views, and mindsets.
- Use what you know for choices at school and work.
- Discuss language and voice and how and why they affect options.
- Complete a community resource project.

$$R + R + R = R + R + R^{Ruby}$$

The little rule above states that if there is no relationship or understanding of the rules and regulations an individual is forced to live with, problems will arise. There are rules everywhere. Schools have rules, businesses have rules, and families have rules. They are the norms of behavior we accept and live by. Generally, individuals follow rules because of a relationship with a person or because following the rules will allow them to connect to a goal or outcome. For example, a teenager follows the rules used at home because he values the relationship with his family. At work following rules is relative to keeping a job and maintaining safety.

When an individual doesn't know the rules of a group or uses a different set, misunderstandings and resentment may occur. People often think everyone knows and uses the same set of rules they do. When an individual uses different rules, there is an assumption that the person is either rude or not very smart, and the reaction may be anger or resistance. Consider a stranger walking up to you and telling you to get a haircut. The response would be resentment, refusal, or worse. But if someone you have a relationship with—like your girlfriend, your mother, or your boss—were to ask you to cut your hair, the response would probably be different. Rules + Rigor + Relationship = Resources + Results + Respect. Use this pattern to sort options, make decisions, and reframe the information to the power of you!

$$R + R + R = R + R + R^{YOU}$$

Rules WITHOUT a Relationship = Resentment + Refusal + Rebellion + Resistance + Rework + Regret
Rules WITH a Relationship = Resources + Respect + Resilience + Reasons + Results + Relevance

Relationships drive actions. They are the reason: the what, why, and how we do things. Generally relationships are associated with people, but relationships can also be the connections to a goal or future picture. An example of a personal relationship: You learn sign language because someone important in your life cannot hear, but you still want to communicate with that person. An example of a relationship to a goal: Learning math in a class you don't like because the math is connected to reaching your goal of being a certified mechanic on the NASCAR circuit. The ability to see relationships between activities and future outcomes can be used to help you get through difficult situations.

What, Why, and How: Three Steps in a Learning Process

> ### WHAT will I learn from *The R Rules?*
> Information, strategies, and tools to identify,
> increase, and use resources.

> ### WHY would I want to learn this?
> Resources influence the way we think, behave, and learn.
> They are important factors for success in life, at school, and at work.
> All people are problem solvers, face unique challenges,
> have varying degrees of resources, and use
> the resources they have to meet those challenges.

> ### HOW will using this benefit me?
> Use information and tools in *The R Rules* to identify and increase resources,
> understand realities, patterns, and hidden rules used in different economic environments,
> and learn information and strategies for seeing options and choices, developing a future
> picture, and making a positive difference in your life and the lives of others.

Why are resources so important? Success or failure at school and work is often related to the resources—or a lack of them—that are available to an individual. Consider a student who would like to participate in an after-school program, sport, or has been hired for a job, but lacks a key resource like transportation. We often think of resources only in terms of finances. Money is one resource and can be used to purchase goods or services, but other resources are just as important in order to live well. Resources like language, personal strength, know-how, relationships, and understanding social cues—hidden rules—are all resources and greatly influence outcomes. Consider David's resources as you read the story below. We all have a set of resources. Like David, it may be necessary to rethink or develop resources that can be added to the ones that are currently available in order to accomplish a task or reach a goal.

David was a thin young man with dark eyes and a presence beyond his 16 years. Throughout the training he sat quietly, listening and taking notes. As I finished my presentation and was preparing to leave, David approached to ask a question.

Grade Court is a program that offers juvenile offenders the opportunity to trade cell time for hours in the classroom working toward graduation requirements. Certified teachers provide instruction and monitor the progress of the participants, who report to the court on a regular basis. Our program worked with Grade Court and had just provided a one-day session on organizational skills and goal setting. The following week, all of the students would complete a tour of the local college.

David asked if I worked at the college. I explained my connection and inquired as to how I might help. He told me that he was close to completing his Grade Court hours and was preparing for the General Educational Development Test (GED). When he received his GED, the college would give him a scholarship. His question: How do you register for classes at the college? A call to the college set up a meeting for David. On the day scheduled for the tour, someone from admissions would meet with him and help him through the maze of registration.

On Friday the bus came to the school, and all of the students, anxious for the trip, quickly boarded—all of the students except one. David was not there. We waited, no air conditioning on the bus, temperature rising, faith dropping. We waited five minutes. Then ten. All the kids knew how important this was to David, and they asked to wait another five minutes, then another each time I wanted to leave. As the old blue car chugged into the parking lot, there was a collective sigh of relief. David, black hair glistening and tied back, dressed in a new, navy blue T-shirt, gold chain, Levis with a crease, and tennis shoes scrubbed white, boarded the bus.

David met with the director of admissions at the college that day. He enrolled and has been taking classes for the past two years working to earn an associate's degree. He is going to be a graphic designer.

I learned later how hard David worked to make it to that college tour. Early in the week David's mother had a crisis, and he had to drive 35 miles to the hospital where she qualifies to receive free medical services. David completed his Grade Court hours and passed his GED exam. He also had to work extra hours at his part-time job because his baby was sick. Medicare would pay the hospital fees; David had to find money for the prescriptions.

Failure at school and work is often due to a lack of resources or missing resources needed to complete a specific task or goal. Each of us has resources, but typically resources are thought of only in terms of finances. While finances are extremely important, success or failure is often dependent on other resources and how they are used. David had some resources, but in order to reach his goal and succeed at school, new resources were needed. For David, a relationship that could provide the information to register for college was the missing resource.

The R Rules explores hidden rules and mindsets relative to different economic realities and environments; resources, relationships, and why they have such a big impact on success at school and work; tools and processes to see patterns, relationships, and connections that identify and increase resources and choices; and ways to build and reach future pictures and win more often.

Resources are related or connected. Each resource has an influence on all of the others. Emotional and mental resources affect how financial resources are used. Like a line of dominoes, if one falls, it will cause another to fall, then another. This relationship is a cause and effect pattern. Understanding resources and patterns will help you see connections for predicting and planning. Use this mental model to sort possibilities and create a picture to see patterns, predict, and plan.

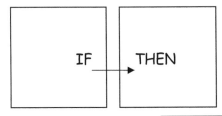

Economic Realities: The actual state of resources, including money, available to an individual.
Mental Model: To translate the concrete to the abstract, the mind holds information in a mental model—a picture, story, metaphor, or analogy. Mental models show the structure, pattern, or purpose.

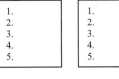

Use a different color to highlight if/then in stories.
IF this happens, *THEN* this will or could happen ...
If she says ...————————➜ then I'll say ...
If we are going to the party,——➜ then ...
If I ask George out, ————➜ then ...
If the baby cries, ————————➜ then ...

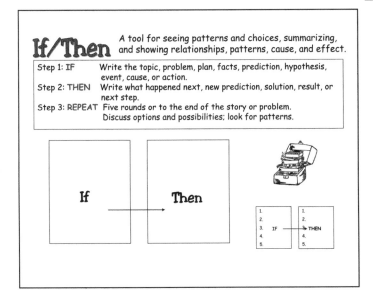

If/Then   A tool for seeing patterns and choices, summarizing, and showing relationships, patterns, cause, and effect.

Step 1: IF   Write the topic, problem, plan, facts, prediction, hypothesis, event, cause, or action.
Step 2: THEN   Write what happened next, new prediction, solution, result, or next step.
Step 3: REPEAT Five rounds or to the end of the story or problem. Discuss options and possibilities; look for patterns.

If ➜ Then

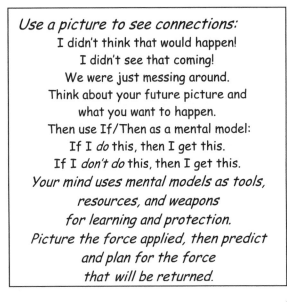

Use a picture to see connections:
I didn't think that would happen!
I didn't see that coming!
We were just messing around.
Think about your future picture and what you want to happen.
Then use If/Then as a mental model:
If I *do* this, then I get this.
If I *don't do* this, then I get this.
Your mind uses mental models as tools, resources, and weapons for learning and protection. Picture the force applied, then predict and plan for the force that will be returned.

Can you read this? Olny srmat poelpe can.

I cluod not blveiee taht I cluod aulaclty uesdnatnrd waht I was rdaineg. Aoccdrnig to rscheearch at Cmabrigde Uinervtisy, it deosn't mttaer in waht oredr the ltteers in a wrod are, the olny iprmoatnt tihng is taht the frist and lsat ltteer be in the rghit pclae. The rset can be a taotl mses and you can sitll raed it wouthit a porbelm. Tihs is bcuseae the huamn mnid deos not raed ervey lteter by istlef, but mkaes cnnocetions to pttaerns of the wrod as a wlohe. Amzanig, huh? Yaeh, and I awlyas tghuhot slpeling was the msot ipmorantt prat of rdanieg.

The R Rules will ask you to stretch your thinking, to think "out of the box," to consider new ideas, uncover hidden rules, and view patterns that often remain unnoticed. Thinking out of the box connects new realities and information to old understandings, increasing knowledge and resources. The ability to see patterns allows individuals to sort information, see new options and possibilities, predict and plan, increase choices, and win more often at the game of life.

 Think

Use what, why, and how to sort information and see relationships:

WWH

A tool for sorting and using information and identifying relationships and patterns.

Step 1: What — Points out the stimulus—the information, topic, or focus.
Step 2: Why — States why the information is or is not important or relevant. *Explains* the meaning, consequences, or relationship.
Step 3: How — Provides a strategy to answer the first two questions. How can or will the answers to the *what* and *why* be used?

What	Why	How

What: Rules and regulations
Why: Relationship to self, goal, future
How: Response based on how important the relationship, or why, is to you

A Mental Model:

To think out of the box …
use all three boxes:
What, Why, and How

Relationships = Reasons

Dr. James Comer: "No significant learning occurs without a significant relationship."
Think of relationships in your life, why they are important, and how they inspire and help you reach goals, learn, and live well.

MORE ⬚ Think

A little quiz

1. If something occurs *most of the time*, it occurs _____?_____% of the time.

2. If you say to someone on the phone that you will do something *right away*, you will do it within how long?

3. If you say to someone that you are sort of busy, but you will get to it *as soon as possible*, you will do it within how long?

4. If you are invited to dinner at a friend's house, what time of the day will you be having a meal?

5. I introduce you to my grandpa. How are we related?

6. Draw a Girafopotamus.

> To live and communicate in the larger society, common language and definitions are used. Are there hidden rules?

Adapted from the work of Janet Peregoy

Success:

Do you see relationships, patterns, or hidden rules?

Language and words are tools of the mind.
Language is necessary for communication and negotiation.

Use the following as checklists to develop personal resources.

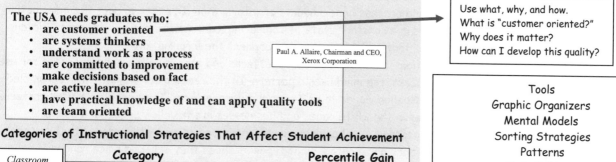

R Rule References

The USA needs graduates who:
- are customer oriented
- are systems thinkers
- understand work as a process
- are committed to improvement
- make decisions based on fact
- are active learners
- have practical knowledge of and can apply quality tools
- are team oriented

Paul A. Allaire, Chairman and CEO, Xerox Corporation

Use what, why, and how.
What is "customer oriented?"
Why does it matter?
How can I develop this quality?

Categories of Instructional Strategies That Affect Student Achievement

Classroom Instruction That Works Marzano, Pickering, Pollock

Category	Percentile Gain
Identifying similarities and differences	45
Summarizing and note taking	34
Reinforcing effort and providing recognition	29
Homework and practice	28
Nonlinguistic representations	27
Cooperative learning	27
Setting objectives and providing feedback	23
Generating and testing hypotheses	23
Questions, cues, and advance organizers	22

www.21stcenturyskills.org
www.doleta.gov

To improve these skills use ⟶

Tools
Graphic Organizers
Mental Models
Sorting Strategies
Patterns
Data Folders
Goal Setting and Action Plans
Planning Backwards
Sketching and Cartooning
Quotations
Teamwork
Role Models
Sequence, Time, and Step Charts
Self-Talk
Rubrics
Question Making
Formal Register

How do you define success at SCHOOL and WORK?

Each of the skills listed on the chart is a resource identified as necessary in order to be successful and respected in the workplace. How important are these same skills at school?

Rate yourself: ⟶
In the column to the right, rate yourself on each skill. Use a scale of 1 to 5. 5 is the highest, 1 the lowest.

Next, ask someone you trust to rate you. Compare ratings and discuss the numbers.

Make a plan:
Increase or develop one or two of these skills. First check your resources. Next write a SMART goal, then a SMART action plan.

Remember:
Procedural Self-Talk
Positive Self-Talk
Positive Role Models
Relationships of Mutual Respect
Resources
Future Picture

21st-Century Skills:
Critical thinking, information analysis, problem solving, analytical thinking, creativity, innovation, communication, collaboration, global awareness, social responsibility, business, entrepreneurial, and information and communications technology literacy, all in the context of modern life.

Rate these skills in the order of importance for each time period.

Work Skills	1990	2010
Teamwork		
Problem Solving Skills		
Interpersonal Skills		
Verbal Communication		
Listening		
Personal Development		
Creative Thinking		
Leadership and Self Motivation		
Goal Setting		
Writing		
Technology and Media Skills		
Effective Organization		
Computation Skills		
Reading		
Understanding of Systems		

How are these skills different at school and work? How are they alike?

Three qualities of a leader are:

Examples of interpersonal skills are:

Patterns   99 + 99 + 99 + 99 + 99 =

Patterns are sets that repeat over and over again. They come in many forms: shapes, numbers, sounds, and behaviors. Individuals constantly gather and process huge amounts of information. In order to sort the information, the mind uses patterns. The mind is always in a constant state of comparing, contrasting, and sorting facts, details, and information to determine what is important, what is not, and to connect the information.

Once the mind sorts the information, it is organized using patterns and stored so it can be accessed for use in the future. To complete any task or process, the mind uses a pattern. In the reading activity with the scrambled words, the mind is able to connect the misspelled words to patterns and decode them. The phone book uses patterns like listing names alphabetically, residences in the white pages and businesses in the yellow pages, and so on.

Patterns are used to shop. The process of purchasing a pair of shoes begins by sorting stores that sell shoes from those that don't, determining where they are located, what types of shoes they sell, and price ranges. At the store it will be necessary to locate the shoe department, then find the size, style, and price. The process will be repeated each time a new store is visited.

Patterns show relationships and help us understand the reasons for an activity. For example, individuals study mathematical patterns in order to assign order and value to the universe. The pattern in algebra is to solve for unknowns through equations. Geometry uses logic to order and assign values to forms and space.

The brain gathers and sorts information using the senses: sight, sound, smell, touch, taste. This information is referred to as sensory information. The mind uses patterns for location and order; the Big Dipper is a way to locate and give order to certain stars in the night sky. A pattern is used to locate groups of students who always sit or gather in the same place. Geese fly in a V formation or pattern for increased efficiency. When individuals look at someone's face, they are processing about 29,000 pieces of sensory information into patterns that allow them to identify the person they are seeing. These are sensory patterns because they are gathered using the senses.

To store and connect information in the mind, the brain reframes the sensory information into abstract information called mental images or mental models. Mental models are a picture, a story, a metaphor, or analogy, and show the structure, pattern, or purpose. A globe of the world is an example of a mental model because it provides a picture of the earth and the patterns of water, land, etc.

Other abstract representations, such as letters and words, formulas, and numbers, are used to translate sensory patterns into mental models. An example is heat. Actual heat is determined by touch and feel; translated into an abstract form, it becomes a number of degrees Fahrenheit. Mental models are a way the mind sorts, translates, and holds information so it can be accessed. If you can see the patterns, you can predict. If you can predict, you can plan. If you can plan, you can build resources to play the game and win more often.

List as many patterns as you can related to:

time	alike and different	geography	classifications
vehicles	habits	rules	games
a baby	jobs	writing	training a pet
outlines	relationships	taking a test	living things
task steps	writing	computers	cooking
clothes	music	books	mathematics

Game Day Rules

A pattern to see patterns:
What is the cause, event, or parts, and do they repeat?
Why is this important?
How can I use this knowledge to learn, win, and get ahead?

R + R − R = R + R
R + R + R = R + R + R

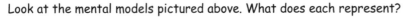

Look at the mental models pictured above. What does each represent?

Use learning patterns. Patterns allow details and information to be grouped or chunked to see the big picture, reason, or concept. This allows knowledge to be transferred from one situation to another and to be compared to see similarities, differences, and repeating patterns. Consider this story about Diane's daughter and a Civil War unit in school:

One night Diane returned home after a trip. Her daughter greeted her and shared that her class had just finished its six-week unit on the Civil War. During the unit the class learned details about the war and completed several activities, including a salt map, reports on Union and **Confederate** generals, virtual tours of battlefields, definitions of vocabulary terms, two book reports—they even attended school dressed as a person who lived during the Civil War. They learned a lot about *WHAT* happened during the Civil War. The conversation when Diane arrived home went like this:

"Guess what, Mom? We finished our Civil War unit today! Guess what my grade was!"

"I don't know. Tell me."

"I got an A+."

"Good for you! I bet you learned a lot!"

"Well, I am glad about the grade, but there's one thing I don't understand. Mom, why did they fight the Civil War?"

The *what* was all of the details, activities, events, and vocabulary words related to the Civil War.

The *why*, the big concept, purpose, or reason to study the Civil War, was to understand that there was a conflict between states regarding their individual rights. This pattern repeats in history, and it is important to understand that different cultures and groups have varying ideas and beliefs, and often conflicts arise.

The *how* to use this information is to understand that patterns repeat in history so the concept that people often disagree and conflicts arise can be used to understand, compare, and contrast other conflicts and wars to past, present, and future pictures.

Ask: *What* is the big concept or pattern; *why* is it important; *how* can this be used to see similar patterns, predict what will happen, and plan a response?   If this occurs ⟶ then

---

A pattern: Give a person a fish and that person will eat for a day. Teach a person to fish and that person will eat for a lifetime.

Give a person facts and details and that person can use them today. Teach a person patterns and that person can use them for a lifetime.

Do you have personal patterns?

Time: Draw a timeline showing every year of your life. List one important event for each year. Or, keep a log for 14 days and record how long it takes you to complete a particular task each day, such as getting ready for school, doing homework, getting to work, etc.

Space: List the places you spend most of your time or go most often for fun.

Behaviors: Do your friends all have the same interests you do? Do you generally arrive early, on time, or late?

Style: Favorite music, clothing type, transportation.

Music: Type, artist, group.

Maintenance: Eat regularly, schedule hair care, get regular medical checkups, and exercise.

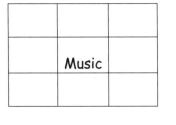

Write an occupation in the center square, then list patterns that would be observed and provide important information for each.
Examples: Doctor, construction worker, police officer, pilot, teacher, investor, mechanic, waitress, athlete.

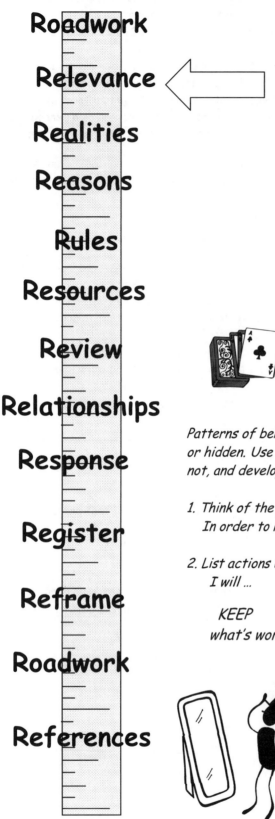

Roadwork

Relevance

Realities

Reasons

Rules

Resources

Review

Relationships

Response

Register

Reframe

Roadwork

References

What did you learn?
Why is it important?
How can you use it?

Check the cards in your hand.
Which cards will you keep, discard, or draw?

Patterns of behavior develop over time. They are automatic and often unseen or hidden. Use the list to check patterns, sort what is working from what is not, and develop strategies to increase resources.

1. Think of the goal or future picture:
In order to reach my goal of_____,

2. List actions under each of the categories below that will help you get there.
I will ...

KEEP	START	STOP
what's working	what will help or is needed	what is not helping or unnecessary

Seeing and using patterns is a resource.
Explain how the ability to see patterns is a resource for learning.
Check the cards in your hand. How can they be improved, combined, and used to win?

Notes

Chapter 3
REALITIES: Get Real

What it is: A reality is what is real, the actual current state of affairs or true condition, the set of facts or mental model that an individual uses everyday, the set of beliefs based on the patterns, stories, and mindsets used by the individual. Using these definitions of reality, read the following statements and point out the factors that influence the "reality" in each of them: 1) A man found a painting in his attic. He knew it was worth a lot of money, so he sold it for 100 coins. He is rich. 2) A young man's family members love and care for him. 3) I need to be in another state by five o'clock tomorrow. 4) No one in my family has ever attended college. 5) Green is my friend's favorite color. If I buy her something green, she will like it.

Why this is important: Realities are important because they influence the way we act, think, and learn. Realities are the set of facts, mental models, or patterns individuals use to sort and understand information and respond. They are what we base our actions and plans on. Understanding various realities can help you understand viewpoints and reasons different than your own.

How you can use this information: Understanding others' realities will enable you to interact with them in mutually beneficial ways. Understanding your own reality and the patterns you use to make choices will help you see choices and can give a new meaning or purpose to your work. Here is an example:

Consider the following realities:

*What is the **pattern** or reality of education and earnings?*

Level of Education	Annual Earnings	Hourly Earnings
Bachelor's Degree	$35,594	$19.56
Associate's Degree	$26,536	$14.58
High School Graduate	$18,571	$10.20
High School Dropout	$10,839	$5.95

New Mexico Department of Labor, 2002

THINK

Use these figures to see a pattern:
A high school graduate earns $10 per hour, on average.
A high school dropout earns $6 per hour, on average.
The difference in earnings between a high school graduate and a high school dropout:
$10 – $6 = $4 more earned by the graduate for each hour worked.
Forty hours (average work week) × $4 per hour = $160 more per week.
Fifty work weeks per year (assuming two weeks vacation) × $160 = $8,000 more earned each year.
Fifty years × $8,000 = $400,000 more during a lifetime.

So how much is staying in school worth to you?
There are 1,080 hours in one school year.
If you are currently in tenth grade, you have three more years X 1,080 hours, or 3,240 hours.
$400,000 divided by 3,240 hours = $123 per hour. Is $400,000 in the future worth your time now?

Does this reality make you feel better or think differently about getting a formal education? Seeing different realities can help you see patterns, reasons, different viewpoints, and options. Having a different reality, like a future picture you want to reach, can help you decide how to respond to a situation or person. Use a What, Why, and How to check realities. Consider homework. The reality is that to learn a skill, practice is required. Great athletes practice. Homework is assigned so great minds have time to practice. *Understanding the connection between the reason or reality and the intended benefit can help you see meaning or purpose. R + R – R = R + R*

What are you building? What is your reality?
Money is one resource. Hope and purpose are resources.

A budget provides a record, helps you see how your money is being spent and where you can save, and is a tool to help understand finances, see patterns, make decisions, predict, plan, and save.

Activity: How much do you need to live for one month?

Complete the following worksheet.

40 hours a week x $6 per hour = _____ per week

Monthly salary (weekly salary x 4 weeks) = _____ per month

Less cost of one-bedroom apartment per month _____ = amount you now have _____

Less food for one person for one month _____ = amount you now have _____

Less utilities for one month _____ = amount your now have _____

Less car payment + insurance + gasoline _____ = amount you now have _____

Less Laundromat _____ = amount you now have _____

Less clothing, school supplies, medical, makeup _____ = amount you now have _____

Telephone, cable television, and Internet access _____ = amount you now have _____

Less taxes (about $80 per month) = _____. This amount is your disposable income, or the money that you have left over to spend every month. A fixed expense means the amount is the same each month. The amount of a variable expense changes. A periodic expense is one that doesn't occur every month.

Weekly allowance _____ x 52 weeks = _____ $

After-school job _____ x 36 weeks = _____ $

School break/summer jobs _____ x 16 weeks = _____ $

Gifts of money _____ $

Other _____ $_____

Total income: $

Complete the activity above by checking the newspaper, Internet, and local sources to learn the average cost and location of housing and the price of vehicles and food in your area. Learn what types of jobs are available and the average salaries. Consider options that will make your money go further: roommates, two jobs, public transportation, a trust fund, or assistance. Now repeat the activity, but change the figure on the first line from $6 to $10. That is what the average high school graduate earns per hour. Does this change your reality about staying in school?

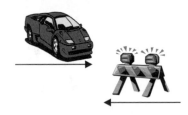

Payday loan: 42% interest
$100 + $42 = $142
Credit Card: 18% interest plus $35 late fee, plus over-limit fee
$100 + $18 + $35 + $35 = $188

Simple interest: dollar amount x interest rate x length of time in years = amount
Compound interest:
original dollar amount + earned interest x interest rate x length of time = amount

Which would you choose?
$100 for one month or 1¢ doubled daily for a month?
What are the local interest rates in your area? Are they the same all across the country?
Are relationships a driver or roadblock when it comes to managing your money?
Many states are passing laws raising the minimum wage. Do you agree or disagree with this?
Use a Force Field tool to show drivers and barriers for mandating a higher minimum wage.
View video: People Like Us, Tammy Crabtree segment. Discuss patterns, realities, and options.

BANKING ...

How much do you know? Match terms to definitions.

_____ 1.	Money the bank lends to use now and pay back later
_____ 2.	Explains the bank fee, charges, interest paid, and minimum balance required
_____ 3.	Two items that are very important when writing a check
_____ 4.	A process to cancel a check after it has been given or mailed
_____ 5.	A form of currency that is purchased and can be replaced if lost or stolen
_____ 6.	Kept on file at bank; used as a way to check or prove who is writing checks
_____ 7.	Form used to keep track of the balance on a checking account
_____ 8.	Signing the back of the check that is written to you so it can be cashed
_____ 9.	Term for the fee or rate charged on a loan
_____ 10.	Terms for ways employers can pay salaries or wages to employees
_____ 11.	Money taken out of wages to pay taxes and insurance
_____ 12.	A check that can be purchased
_____ 13.	Checking the balance on your check register against the bank statement
_____ 14.	A fee paid to the customer for keeping money in a savings account
_____ 15.	Can be used like a check to access money in a checking account
_____ 16.	Form used to put money in a checking or savings account
_____ 17.	Term used by the bank stating there was not enough money in the account

a. credit
b. check register
c. deposit slip
d. interest
e. endorse
f. traveler's check
g. paycheck or direct deposit
h. signature card
i. type of account
j. stop payment
k. interest
l. payroll deduction
m. dollar amount
n. money order
o. cashier's check
p. insufficient funds
q. debit or ATM card
r. reconciliation
s. signature
t. loan

Which bank and type of account are best for Beth and George?

College Account	Basic Account	Prime Timer Account
$100 minimum to open	$100 minimum to open	$100 minimum to open
No minimum balance	No minimum balance	Minimum balance $4,000
No interest earned	No interest earned	Monthly fee: $25, waived with minimum balance
Online statements free	Online statements free	3% interest if balance at or above minimum
No monthly fee	No monthly fee	Check card: $29 per year
Check card: $1 per month	Check card: no fee	Free services: checks, IRA, money orders, online statement, safety deposit box
	Overdraft protection	
	Direct deposit	

Credit Card

_____

BETH	GEORGE
Will open her account with a $100 deposit	Will open his account with a $1,500 deposit
Writes ten checks a month	Writes 50 checks a month
Works from 8 a.m. to 7 p.m. Monday–Saturday	Works 8 a.m. to 5 pm Monday–Friday
Uses public transportation	Drives past Citizens Bank every day
Gets paid every other Saturday	Checks his account online weekly
Plans errands to save time and bus fare	Goes to his safety deposit box regularly
Goes to the bank every payday, deposits check, and gets enough cash to last until next payday	Travels and goes to the bank to cash large checks
	Salary is $5,000 a month

Debit Card

_____

Citizens Bank	First American
Nearest location is a full-service bank	Nearest location offers limited services: check cashing, deposits, withdrawals
Lobby is open Monday–Friday, 9 a.m. to 4 p.m.	Open seven days a week, 8 a.m. to 7 p.m.
Saturday: 10 a.m. to noon	Located inside a grocery store
Drive-through open Mon. to Fri., 9 a.m. to 7 p.m.	No drive-through banking services
Saturday: 9 a.m. to 1 p.m.	Online banking services available
Offers online access	

Individuals receive paychecks on different schedules. Compare budgeting and payment options if an individual is paid once a month, every two weeks, or every week. What are advantages to using automatic withdrawal and deposit? What are benefits of credit and debit cards? How are they different and alike? What services do financial institutions in your area offer? Complete a web search and share information. Remember: .edu = education; .com = commercial; .org = organization; .gov = government. Why is this important?

Review the example. Reframe each amount as it would appear on a check.

$49.93 is written *forty-nine and 93/100*

$24.61 _____

$982.31 _____

$2,742

Rule of 72: *How long will it take to double your money or your debt?*
Divide the number 72 by the interest rate
If you are earning 6% on an investment
72 divided by 6 = 12 years to double
Your credit card charges 24% interest
72 divided by 24 = 3 years to double debt

Write the following checks:
$42.98 to the phone company
$63.42 to the grocery store
$350 to the loan company for the house payment
$3,432 to the IRS to pay income taxes
$19 to the babysitter
$424 to MasterCard. Pay using an electronic check

Name the parts of a check:

1. _____ 2.
3. _____ 4. _____
5. _____
6. _____ 7. _____
8. 9. 10.

George and Beth both owe $2,000 on their credit cards.
Beth manages to pay the minimum monthly payment and an additional $10 each month on the principal.
George pays only the minimum payment each month. At this rate it will take Beth 7 years to pay off her $2,000 balance if she doesn't make any new purchases. It will take George 15 years to pay off his $2,000.
Check your credit card statement; monthly finance rates can change depending on payment history, introductory interest rates, etc. Resource = Choices
Resources: www.Oprah.com
Student Financial Handbook at www.bankofamerica.com
Money Math: Lessons for Life at www.publicdebt.treas.gov/mar/moneymath.htm
Stock Market Game at www.smgww.org
Building Homes of Our Own at www.nahb.org
Money skills at www.visa.ca/moneyskills

Credit Card Realities
Annual Percentage Rate (APR)
Type of interest
Annual fee
Interest on purchases or balance
Over limit fee
Late fee
Does the interest rate change?
Payment date
Grace period

Deposit slips are used to put money into your account. Personalized deposit slips are in the back of the check packet, generic deposit slips are available at the bank.
Complete two deposit slips using the information shown.

Your name	Coin
Your address	Currency
Your city, state, zip code	Checks
Date	Subtotal $
	Less cash $
Signature required for withdrawals	Total $
Name of bank and logo	
123456789---123-0000000	

Make the following deposit.
Use today's date.
17 pennies
6 nickels
15 dimes
16 quarters
15 $1 bills
2 $5 bills
2 $20 bills
$23.98 check, San Juan Spring
$14.96 check, Chandler Motor

Make the following deposit.
Use tomorrow's date.

Check for $547.89
Check for $43.58
Withdraw $40 cash

Checking Accounts

1. You have a beginning balance of $723.86 on January 27. (How did you determine this balance?)
2. On January 28 you purchased groceries at the Piggly Wiggly and wrote check number 204 for $23.98.
3. February 1: paid your rent with check number 205 for $325
4. February 3: deposited your paycheck, $387.25
5. February 4: paid the electric bill to the City of Farmington, check 206 for $73.43
6. February 4: bought gasoline at Amigo Gas Station, paid with debit card, $23.98
7. February 10: went to a show, used debit card, $15
8. February 11: ordered checks, fee was deducted by an automatic payment of $7
9. February 12: paid bills to PNM: $154; Comcast: $43.26; Quest: $48.79; Life Insurance: $25.15
10. February 15: car payment was automatically deducted from you checking account, $193.00
11. February 17: called the bank to check balance on account, and the balance was $486.00
12. *What is the balance in this checking account as of February 17?*

Codes: AD: Automatic Deposit **AP:** Automatic Payment **ATM:** Automated Teller Machine **DC:** Debit Card **EC:** Electronic Check

Check Number	Date	Transaction Description	√	Check/Fee Amount (-)	Deposit Amount (+)	Balance
				$	$	$

Reconciling or *balancing* your checkbook means to compare the balance you show in your check register to the balance the bank shows. Once a month use the paper bank statement you receive in the mail or go online and print one off, then put a mark in your checkbook by each transaction listed on the bank statement. List any transactions that are not listed either in your checkbook or by the bank on the statement. Use the following form to list adjustments and corrections:

Your checkbook balance	$_____	Balance on bank statement	$_____
Deposits not in checkbook	$_____	Deposits not on statement	$_____
Add for total	$_____		$_____
Service charges	$_____	Add for total	$_____
Overdraft charges	$_____		
ATM not listed	$_____	Subtract:	
Checks not listed	$_____	Total outstanding checks	$_____
Other items	$_____		
Subtract total	$_____		
Adjusted balance	$_____	**Adjusted Balance**	$_____

Outstanding Checks		
Check Number	Amount	
Total		

Is it necessary to record transactions and reconcile to the bank statement
if you have electronic access to your checking account?
What is the process to get electronic access or use online banking?
What are the advantages to online banking?

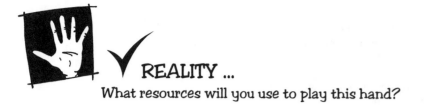

REALITY ...
What resources will you use to play this hand?

You are paid once a month. Paychecks are given out on the first workday of each month.

Your car payment is due on the 15th of each month. You are paid on the 15th of each month. Sometimes you can't make it to the bank on the 15th before closing time to make the payment. Your bank offers a direct deposit service. If you direct deposit, the bank will allow you to write checks on your paycheck before it is deposited and pay back the money with interest.

You deposit your paycheck each week on the day you receive it and keep out enough cash for the week. You never have enough money to pay your bills, but you need spending money.

You want to save money, but your family needs a lot of help. Everyone knows when you are paid, and sometimes they wait for you after work.

You can only put $5 in savings each week. It is such a small amount that you spend it. It is so hard to get ahead anyway, and it feels good to buy something once in a while.

You have a credit card, but are concerned you will overspend.

Your boy-/girlfriend really needs to borrow some money. He/she still owes you from the last time you loaned him/her money and probably won't pay you back this time either.

You balance your checking account every month, but you have been overdrawn three times. You use a debit card and write checks.

To get ready for this job, I might want to:		
Start:	Stop:	Keep:

1. Careers or jobs of interest:

_____
_____
_____
_____
_____
_____
_____
_____
_____
_____
_____
_____

2. Gather information by asking:

What	Why	How

_____
_____
_____
_____
_____

www.careerpathway.org   www.msncareerbuilder.com
www.careerclusters.org   www.dol.state.nm.us
www.careervoyages.gov   www.salary.com
www.federaljobsearch.com

Check at least three resources:
Book, magazine, newspaper, Internet, college,
businesses, trade schools, Department of Labor.
Others:

3. I might want to walk a mile in these shoes …

_____
_____
_____
_____

4. Drivers   Barriers

5. Consider options:

If	→	Then

1._____
2._____
3._____
4._____
5._____
6._____

6. Write a plan.

Who What	Why	How	Results	When

_____
_____
_____
_____
_____

Plan Backwards

Date to review progress:_____

Career survey: How well do you know yourself?

Give yourself one point for each item that applies to you.

ACTIVITIES THAT SOUND INTERESTING

1. Reading or writing stories or articles
2. Designing and building scenery for plays
3. Taking photographs
4. Acting in a play or movie
5. Listening to/playing music
6. Designing clothing, brochures, or posters

MY PERSONAL QUALITIES

1. Imaginative
2. Creative
3. Outgoing
4. Expressive
5. Performer

IN MY FREE TIME I WOULD ENJOY

1. Working on the school paper or yearbook
2. Acting in a play or video
3. Painting pictures, murals, and drawing
4. Broadcasting a sporting event

SCHOOL SUBJECTS/ACTIVITIES I ENJOY AND DO WELL IN

1. Social Studies 2. Choir, Symphony, Band
3. Creative Writing 4. Art 5. Drama
6. Drafting 7. Public Speaking

TOTAL NUMBER CIRCLED [   ]
CAREER PATH 1

ACTIVITIES THAT SOUND INTERESTING

1. Interviewing people
2. Using computer programs
3. Winning a sales contest
4. Being captain/leader of a team
5. Working with numbers
6. Dealing with money

MY PERSONAL QUALITIES

1. Practical
2. Independent
3. Organized
4. Leader
5. Like to be around people

IN MY FREE TIME I WOULD ENJOY

1. Being in a speech contest or debate
2. Surfing the Internet
3. Designing a website
4. Starting my own business

SCHOOL SUBJECTS/ACTIVITIES I ENJOY AND DO WELL IN

1. Speech 2. Language 3. Math
4. Marketing 5. Accounting 6. Technology
7. Business Math

TOTAL NUMBER CIRCLED [   ]
CAREER PATH 2

ACTIVITIES THAT SOUND INTERESTING

1. Preparing medicine in a pharmacy
2. Helping sick people
3. Working with animals
4. Helping with sports injuries
5. Studying anatomy and diseases
6. Performing surgery

MY PERSONAL STRENGTHS

1. Compassionate and caring
2. Good listener
3. Good at following directions carefully
4. Conscientious and careful
5. Patient

IN MY FREE TIME I WOULD ENJOY

1. Volunteering at a hospital or senior home
2. Taking care of pets
3. Exercising and taking care of myself
4. Working as a trainer on a team

SCHOOL SUBJECTS/ACTIVITIES I ENJOY AND DO WELL IN

1. Math 2. Science 3. Biology 4. Chemistry
5. Communication 6. Spanish/French
6. Health

TOTAL NUMBER CIRCLED [   ]
CAREER PATH 3

ACTIVITIES THAT SOUND INTERESTING

1. Helping people solve problems
2. Working with children
3. Working with elderly people
4. Preparing food
5. Being involved in politics
6. Solving a mystery

MY PERSONAL QUALITIES

1. Friendly
2. Outgoing
3. Good at making decisions
4. Good listener
5. Follow directions

IN MY FREE TIME I WOULD ENJOY

1. Helping solve my friends' problems
2. Helping on a community project
3. Coaching/tutoring
4. Exploring new places

SCHOOL SUBJECTS/ACTIVITIES I ENJOY AND DO WELL IN

1. Language Arts 2. History 3. Speech
4. Math

TOTAL NUMBER CIRCLED [   ]
CAREER PATH 4

ACTIVITIES THAT SOUND INTERESTING

1. Putting things together
2. Designing buildings
3. Working on cars/mechanical things
4. Using advanced math to solve problems
5. Fixing things that are broken
6. Using tools

MY PERSONAL QUALITIES

1. Practical
2. Like using my hands
3. Logical
4. Good at reading manuals
5. Observation

IN MY FREE TIME I WOULD ENJOY

1. Building models
2. Drawing car prototypes
3. Designing mechanical things
4. Inventing a new product

SCHOOL SUBJECTS/ACTIVITIES I ENJOY AND DO WELL IN

1. Math 2. Geometry 3. Woodworking
4. Science 5. Welding

TOTAL NUMBER CIRCLED [   ]
CAREER PATH 5

ACTIVITIES THAT SOUND INTERESTING

1. Being outdoors
2. Predicting and measuring earthquakes
3. Growing flowers, plants, trees
4. Studying rocks and minerals
5. Raising fish or animals
6. Working in a chemistry lab

MY PERSONAL QUALITIES

1. Curious
2. Nature lover
3. Physically active
4. Problem solver
5. Sense of direction

IN MY FREE TIME I WOULD ENJOY

1. Camping
2. Going on a nature trail
3. Experimenting with a chemistry set
4. Mountain climbing

SCHOOL SUBJECTS/ACTIVITIES I ENJOY AND DO WELL IN

1. Math 2. Biology 3. Geography 4. Geometry
5. Physics 6. Horticulture

TOTAL NUMBER CIRCLED [   ]
CAREER PATH 6

Survey (as adapted from Career Partnership, Illinois) reprinted with permission from Marie Schumacher, schumacherma@sanjuancollege.edu, Farmington, New Mexico.

Career Path 1 **ARTS and COMMUNICATIONS** Occupations in this path are related to the humanities, performing, visual, literacy, and media arts. These include architecture, interior design, creative writing, fashion design, film, fine arts, graphic design and production, journalism, languages, radio, television, advertising, and public relations.	**Career Path 2** **BUSINESS, MANAGEMENT, and COMPUTER TECHNOLOGY** Occupations in this path are related to the business environment. These include entrepreneurship, sales, marketing, computer/information systems, finance, accounting, personnel, economics, and management.	**Career Path 3** **HEALTH SERVICES** Occupations in this path are related to the promotion of health and the treatment of disease. These include research, prevention, treatment, and related technologies.
	CAREER PATHS	
Career Path 4 **HUMAN SERVICES** Occupations in this path are related to economic, political, and social systems. These include education, government, law and law enforcement, leisure and recreation, delivery, military, religion, child care, social services, and personal services.	**Career Path 5** **ENGINEERING and INDUSTRIAL TECHNOLOGY** Occupations in this path are related to the technologies necessary to design, develop, install, and maintain physical systems. These include engineering, manufacturing, construction, service, and related technologies.	**Career Path 6** **NATURAL RESOURCES and ENVIRONMENTAL SCIENCES** Occupations in this path are related to agriculture, the environment, and natural resources. They include agricultural sciences, earth science, environmental sciences, fisheries, forestry, horticulture, and wildlife.

Survey (as adapted from Career Partnership, Illinois) used with permission of Marie Schumacher, Farmington, New Mexico.

In the center square of each Lotus Diagram, write a career category that is of most interest to you. Then list the specific field or jobs that relate to the category. Example: Manager—clothing store, automotive parts, financial, etc. Use information generated to consider possible jobs or career clusters on the following pages.

MATCH WHAT YOU SEE DURING A COLLEGE TOUR OR JOB FAIR TO A CAREER CLUSTER LISTED BELOW

What: The categories schools use to organize classes and activities around 16 broad categories that include virtually all occupations from entry level to careers as a professional.

Why: A way to organize information by providing a way to connect what students learn in school with the knowledge and skills they need for success in college, at work, and in careers.

How: Career clusters identify pathways from secondary schools to two- and four-year colleges, graduate school, and the workplace so students can see what they need to learn in school to prepare for the future they want.

The 16 Career Clusters

Agriculture, Food & Natural Resources **1**	The production, processing, marketing, distribution, financing, and development of agricultural commodities and resources including food, fiber, wood products, natural resources, horticulture, and other plant and animal products/resources.
Architecture & Construction **2**	Careers in designing, planning, managing, building, and maintaining the built environment.
Arts, A/V Technology & Communications **3**	Designing, producing, exhibiting, performing, writing, and publishing multimedia content including visual and performing arts and design, journalism, and entertainment services.
Business, Management & Administration **4**	Business management and administration careers encompass planning, organizing, directing, and evaluating business functions essential to efficient and productive business operations. Business management and administration career opportunities are available in every sector of the economy.
Education & Training **5**	Planning, managing, and providing education and training services and related learning support services.
Finance **6**	Planning, services for financial and investment planning, banking, insurance, and business financial management.
Government & Public Administration **7**	Executing governmental functions including governance, national security, foreign service, planning, revenue and taxation, regulation, management, and administration at the local, state, and federal levels.
Health Science **8**	Planning, managing, and providing therapeutic services, diagnostic services, health informatics, support services, and biotechnology research and development.
Hospitality & Tourism **9**	Hospitality and tourism encompasses the management, marketing, and operations of restaurants and other foodservices, lodging, attractions, recreation events, and travel-related services.
Human Services **10**	Preparing individuals for employment in career pathways that relate to families and human needs.

The Career Clusters icons are being used with permission of the States' Career Clusters Initiative, 2007, www.careerclusters.org

Information Technology 11	Entry level, technical, and professional careers related to the design, development, support, and management of hardware, software, multimedia, and systems integration services.
Law, Public Safety, Corrections & Security 12	Planning, managing, and providing legal, public safety, and protective services, and homeland security, including professional and technical support services.
Manufacturing 13	Planning, managing, and performing the processing of materials into intermediate or final products and related professional and technical support activities such as production planning and control, maintenance, and manufacturing/process engineering.
Marketing, Sales & Service 14	Planning, managing, and performing marketing activities to reach organizational objectives.
Science, Technology, Engineering & Mathematics 15	Planning, managing, and providing scientific research and professional and technical services (e.g. physical science, social science, engineering), including laboratory and testing services and research and development services.
Transportation, Distribution & Logistics 16	Planning, management, and movement of people, materials, and goods by road, pipeline, air, rail, and water and related professional and technical support services such as transportation infrastructure planning and management, logistics services, and mobile equipment and facility maintenance.

Three career clusters I am most interested in:

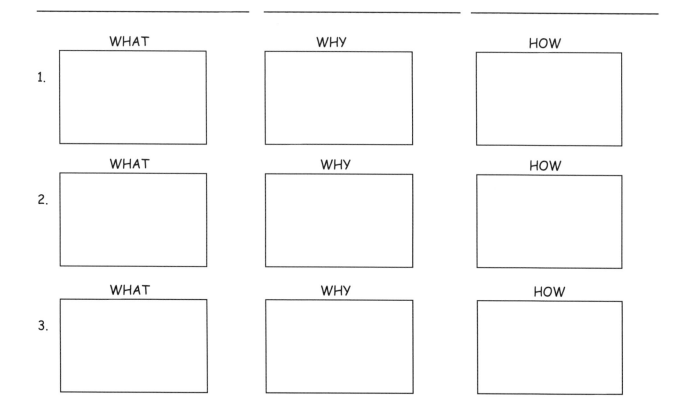

Which shoes would you like to try on?

Veterinarian, $65,000–$86,000
Grocery Store Bagger
Video Game Developer
Professional Skateboarder
Photographer
Stunt Person
CEO
Lifeguard
Sales Associate
Dance Instructor
Embalmer
Lab Technician
Clown
Metropolitan Messenger
Mailman
Bicycle Store Employee
Anthropologist
Baker
Grant Writer
Scientist
Physical Therapist
College Professor
Actor
Hair Stylist, $17,000–$45,000
Legal Secretary
CEO
Opera Singer
Tango Dancer
Voice Coach
Makeup artist
Librarian
Doctor
Anchorperson
Attorney
Judge
Minister
Professor
Scientist
Writer
Journalist
Coroner
Sales Associate
Principal
Concert Pianist
Dentist
Orthodontist
Pharmacist
Physical Therapist
Phlebotomist
Nurse
Teacher
Chef
Salesperson
Prep Cook

Waitress
Photographer
Lab Technician
Scientist
Program Coordinator
Interior Decorator
Software Engineer
Stock Person
Air Traffic Controller
Librarian
Cafeteria Worker
Bomb Squad Expert
Dentist
Detective
Artist
Naturalist
Lighting Specialist
Plastic Surgeon, $220,000–$321,000
Director of Sales
Ranch Hand
Legislative Assistant
Senator
Border Inspector
Home Inspector
Agricultural Engineer
Stockbroker
President
Auctioneer
Safety Manager
Project Inspector
Vintner/Winemaker
Specialty Contractor
Journalist
Environmental Lawyer
Scientist
National Park Ranger
Farmer
Transportation Manager
Salesman
Veterinarian
Parts Manager
Shop Foreman
Anesthesiologist, $205,000–$294,000
Lab Technician
Aerospace Engineer
Sheep Herder
Medical Researcher
Assembly Line Worker
Painter
Pathologist
Reconstructive Surgeon
Medical Examiner
Oral and Maxillofacial Surgeon

Biomedical Engineer
Forensic Pathologist
Surgical Nurse
Medical Assistant
Operating Room Supply Technician
Computer Manufacturer
Ophthalmologist
X-Ray Technician
Emergency Room Staff
CEO, $471,000–$809,000
Stockbroker
Attorney
Judge
Event Coordinator
Opera Singer
Secretary
Ranch Manager, $31,000–$38,000
Travel Agent
Fashion Model
Cosmetic Production
Fashion Designer
Wedding Planner
Senator
Casino Waitress
Sales Associate
Pharmaceutical Representative
Performing Artist
College President
Recording Artist
Journalist
Actress
Funeral Home Director
Receptionist
Financial Analyst
Ski Instructor, $32,000–$55,000
Search and Rescue
Resort Owner
Ski Lift Maintenance
Waiter
Bus Boy
Run Maintenance
Ski Patrol
Babysitter
Camera Operator
Lift Operator
Olympic Athlete
Explorer in the Artic
Sled Driver
Researcher
Forestry Worker
Realtor
Builder

Firefighter, $27,000–$45,000
Aviation Safety Officer
Security Officer
Cargo Inspector
Mining Engineer
Miner
Roustabout
Roughneck
Petroleum Engineer
Geophysicist
Geologist
Fish and Game Officer
Forest Ranger
Logger
Construction Engineer
Freight and Material Movers
Warehouse Manager
Carpenter
General Contractor
Iron-/Metalworker
Machinist/Welder
Boilermaker
Demolition Engineer
Highway Worker
Airline Baggage Handler
Repair Person
Head Nurse, $67,000–$79,000
Physical Therapist
Silversmith
Personal Trainer
Spa Attendant
Banquet Set-up Employee
Hotel Maid
Garbage Collector
Bus Driver
Resort Instructor
Coach
Waitress
Computer Technician
Mail/Package Delivery
Plumber
Massage Therapist
Orthopedic Surgeon
Teacher
Engineer
Gardener
Builder
Musician

Others:

1991 NECESSARY SKILLS: From the 1991 Secretary's Commission on Achieving Necessary Skills

BASIC SKILLS: Reading, writing, arithmetic, listening, speaking,

THINKING SKILLS: creative thinking, decision making, problem solving, visualizing, learns effectively, reasoning

PERSONAL QUALITIES: Responsible, self-esteem, sociability, self-management, integrity, honesty

FIVE COMPETENCIES:

Interpersonal: Works with others, customer oriented, team player, leadership, negotiates, celebrates diversity.

Resource Management: Time, money, materials, facilities, human resources.

Information: Can and does acquire and use information.

Systems: Sees connections, patterns, and how things are interrelated.

Technology: Is able to select, use, and maintain a variety of technologies.

21st-Century Skills

Critical thinking, information analysis, problem solving, analytic thinking, comprehending new ideas, communication, collaboration, and technology literacy, all in the context of modern life.   www.21stcenturyskills.org

Six steps for planning:

1. Assess your personal interests, values, abilities, talents, and resources, and decide what you want to do, be, or have.
2. Evaluate what jobs are projected to be available in the future, requirements for the jobs, and where those jobs are located.
3. Look at specific jobs that are available now and research two companies you are interested in working for.
4. Conduct a school search.
5. Talk to someone who has a job you want or has attended a school you are interested in.
6. Visit the school, company, or job shadow.

www.jobshadow.org

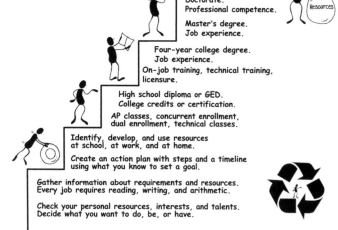

Advanced placement classes
Obtaining a doctorate degree
Having a skill or trade and a formal education
Dual or concurrent enrollment
Attending college

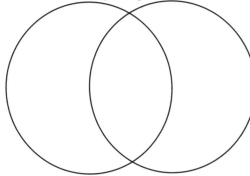

How is college like high school?
    How are they different?
Compare and contrast:
scholarships, grants, loans;
welfare and a scholarship;
GED and high school diploma;
associate's and bachelor's degrees;
certificate and licensure;
career pathways and career clusters;
community college and university.

REALITY CHECK:
*How **many** credits are required for you to graduate?*
How many credits do you currently have?
*What **specific** credits are required to graduate?*

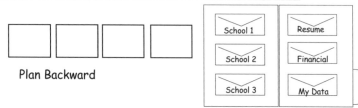

Plan Backward

Get a copy of your current transcript.
Draw your four-year plan in a step chart.
Use as many steps as you need.
Remember: Success is measured one step at time,
and every journey begins with a single step.

TALK THE TALK		
College	GED	Grants
University	ACT	Pell Grant
Community College	SAT	Work Study
Junior College	Early Action	Fellowships
Technical School	Entrance Exam	Concurrent Enrollment
Vocational School	Transcript	Articulated Classes
Graduate School	In-State Tuition	Advanced Placement
Professional School	Tuition	Certification
Public School	College Catalog	Licensure
Private School	Bursar's Office	Associate's Degree
Admissions Office	Registrar's Office	Bachelor's Degree
Admission Requirements	Student Loan	Doctorate
Major	Financial Aid	Reciprocal Agreement
	Scholarships	Competitive Admission

The word *college* is used to describe any education after high school and is subject to interpretation of the individual. A college is an academic institution that offers study programs for students seeking a certificate and/or a two- or four-year degree. A *university* is usually made up of one or more colleges and one or more graduate or professional schools. *Technical institutes, trade, and vocational schools* offer studies mainly in occupational or career fields, and credits are generally not transferable to a four-year degree. Any of these schools may be private or public.

Schools have different admission requirements that may include a specific grade point average, score on an SAT or ACT test, and a resume or essay written by the student. Some colleges consider activities the student has participated in during high school and allow early and competitive admissions.

Course catalogues are free and can be obtained at the school, online, or through the mail. Classes are scheduled on various days and times according to credit hours. Tuition varies from school to school. In-state tuition is the rate students who live in the state where a public school is located pay and is generally much lower than out-of-state tuition. When planning to attend college, include the cost of tuition, books, room, course fees, and food. Some schools have lending libraries for textbooks.

Financial assistance, student loans, scholarships, and work study programs are available, and information can be obtained online, by phone, or by going to the office of admissions or financial aid and asking to see a counselor.

High school students can earn college credits by taking advanced placement classes, taking and passing a test, or by enrolling in dual enrollment or concurrent classes. These are classes that meet college course requirements and can be taken in addition to regular high school classes.

Adapted from New Mexico GEAR UP

School Search: Gather information on three schools that you are interested in. Two schools must be in-state. Take a virtual tour of each. Use an envelope tool and note cards to organize information you record about each school.
Check the following criteria for each school:
1) *Type:* college, trade school, university, private, religious, public; 2) *Location;*
3) *Housing:* on campus and off; 4) *Programs/degrees offered;* 5) *Tuition;* 6) *Financial* assistance, programs, and scholarships; 7) *Admission:* requirements and process; 8) *Student population;*
9) *Student services;* 10) *Technology, library, health center, cafeteria, transportation;*
11) *Class sizes;* 12) *Accreditation;* 13) *Any personal interest.*
Rate the school using a scale of 1 to 5. A rating of 5 is the highest rating, 1 is the lowest.
Request a free copy of a course catalogue or information by e-mail or letter. Develop an action plan.

NEXT STEPS:

- *Fill out a college application.*
- *Get a copy of your transcript.*
- *Fill out a federal loan application.*
  www.fafsa.ed.gov or www.nasfaa.org
- *Check out scholarships and grants.*
- *Develop a resume.*
- *Take SAT or ACT.*
- *Check your class ranking and GPA.*
- *Visit a college, university, and trade school, take online tours, and visit the campus.*

Your business card goes here

LISTED ON A RESUME:

Your name, mailing address, phone number, and e-mail address.

Your career or reason for applying for the job.

Work experience: List your most recent jobs first. Highlight experience that pertains to the job or company to which you are applying. List the employer name, address, dates of employment, and the responsibilities included in your job there.

Education: School name, educational level completed, career pathway, any classes relevant to the job, any extra activities such as clubs, leadership roles, and volunteer work that will help you do the job.

Awards or recognition: Any recognition or award that will show your strengths relative to the job.

References: Names of people who can tell an employer about your qualifications. Get permission from your references first. References can be former employers, teachers, coaches, or peers.

WHAT websites did you visit?

Draw a symbol or picture to represent
JOB, WORK, CAREER

WHY were they helpful? Why were they not helpful?

HOW will you use the information you gathered?

What do you want to do, be, or have?

Why?

How can you make this happen?

When will you make this happen?

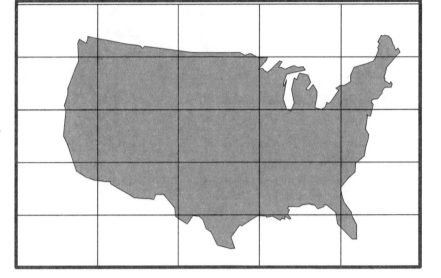

Where?

Consider:

Family, cost of living, weather, transportation, taxes, civic organizations, interests, hobbies, real estate, friends, schools, religion, entertainment.

Other:

Steps:

How will you sort information for your search?
Option: Sort information by region, then state, then city.

What, Why, How   If/Then   Planning Backwards   Force Field   Envelope

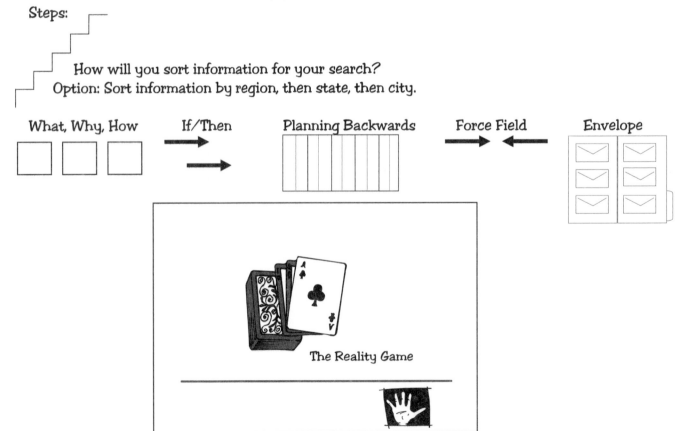

The Reality Game

Today's Reality

Name:	Educational Attainment:
Marital Status: Single _____ Married_____ Widow_____ Divorced_____	Occupation:
Number of Children:	Ages of Children:

Item	Description	+	-	Balance
Monthly Income	Your gross monthly income			
	Spouse's gross monthly income			
	Other income			
	Other income			
	Total gross income			
Payroll Deductions	FICA (Social Security) Tax			
	Federal Withholding Tax			
	State Tax			
	Health/Life Insurance			
	Medicare			
Net Income				
	401K			
	Union Dues			
Bank	Savings			
	Checking			
Housing	Payment or Rent			
	Property Taxes			
	Insurance			
Utilities	Gas			
	Water			
	Electricity			
	Cable			
	Phone			
	Security			
Insurance	Home			
	Automobile			
Transportation				
Childcare				
Food				
Student Loan				
Furniture				
Entertainment				
Charity/Donation				
Travel				
Clothing				
Pets				
Miscellaneous				
Fate:				
Fate:				

It is not just the cards you draw,
but how you play those cards.

CARD OF FATE

What is the current situation?_____

What is the reality of the current situation?_____

_____

Is this important? Why or why not? _____

Do I need to respond? How long can I wait before I respond? How will I respond?

_____

What are possible actions, options, solutions?_____

_____

What resources are available?_____

What resources are missing? _____

Will a different resource work?_____

How can I get this resource?_____

What response will I try?_____

Why will this work?_____

Why won't it work?_____

How will I know it worked?

_____

What else will I try if it doesn't work? Plan B:_____

_____

Consider the following scenarios:

- You are a junior in high school and live with your parents. You are planning to attend a state college when you graduate. You have a job every summer with the city parks department, but do not work during the school year. What resources will you use to go to college?
- You are 16, single with no children, and recently dropped out of high school. You live with your parents, but since you no longer attend school, you have been asked to move out. You need to find an apartment and a job. What are your options?
- You live with a foster family. When you are 18 you will age out of the system. You are 14 now. What resources are available to you?
- You are 17 and the mother of a 6-month-old child. You dropped out of high school. You currently live with your parents, who provide support for you and your child. You worked at a couple of temporary jobs, but caring for your child makes keeping a job very difficult. What resources should you try to develop?

The Resource Project: What resources would help in each of the scenarios above? What is available in your community? Review the resource page in the Reference section. Use the Internet, library, phone book, and other sources to create a list of local, state, and federal agencies that provide assistance and resources

A Reality

The "elephant in the room" is a figure of speech, a term people use to talk about a reality or problem. The reality, like an elephant, is so big that people are forced to deal with it, but no one will call it by name. Everyone knows the elephant is there, but no one wants to talk about it because there is no easy solution. Some people (often the elephants) can't even see the problem, others just ignore it, and others simply can't find the words to talk about it.

Realities are "elephants" that roam through the halls of America's schools. Those realities make a huge difference in the way we think about learning, the time we spend on education, our beliefs and behaviors, and how we are able to respond and participate. A lack of the most basic resources is a reality or "elephant" that many children in America must deal with every day. Economic realities and the patterns and mindsets they create have a huge impact at school and work. Individuals often think their understanding and reality is the only one. Read about the blind men and the elephant to help you further understand and develop a mental model:

Six blind men sought to learn about the elephant. Each took a turn deciding what the elephant was like. The first man leaned against the side of the elephant and told the others the elephant was like a huge, strong wall. The second man felt the elephant's tusk and declared the elephant to be like a spear, round and smooth and sharp. The third man, holding the elephant's squirming trunk, understood the elephant was like a snake. The fourth, holding on to the giant animal's knee, thought the elephant was most like a tree. The fifth, holding the flapping ear, knew the elephant was a giant fan. The sixth, holding the elephant's swinging tail, said the elephant was a rope. Each man used his own experience and argued that his reality was right.

Similar to the patterns and rules in different economic classes, each man in the story had his own reality. Like the blind men, we each come to school and work with different realities and resources. *The R Rules* explores resources, patterns, and the hidden rules of behavior and problem solving used in different economic environments. Like the elephant in the room, they are topics that are often ignored or called by a different name. As in the story, each man had a different viewpoint and mental model of what the elephant looked like.

The R Rules honors the internal assets of people from all economic classes and provides a vocabulary to talk about patterns and different views. The hope is that you will use this information to identify skills, develop resources, and understand realties other than your own as you choose your way, solve problems, and make a difference. As the blind men learned, when information is shared to create a view of the big picture, it can be used for a common effort. When individuals are not willing to share information or use only their reality, it can become a point for argument and division.

Realities:

What: *Facts about economics and status of children in America* (2003 census)

Poverty is defined as the extent to which an individual does without resources.

A child is defined as anyone 18 or under.

People 18 and under are the largest group of people living in poverty in the United States.

One out of every five children in America lives in poverty.

The poverty line is $20,000 per year for a family of four. (2006, NCCP)

The group with the largest **number** of children living in poverty is white.

The group with the largest **percentage** of children in poverty is Native American, followed by African American, followed by Hispanic, then white.

Why: *Factors that influence economic realties:*

Educational attainment of the adults in the home

Addiction issues of adults in the home

Family structure—30% single-parent homes

Immigration

Language issues

Parental employment and earnings of the adults in the home

Reasons individuals leave one economic reality and move to another:

The individuals are able to see their future. Know what they want to be, do, or have.

The individual has a specific skill or talent.

The current reality is too painful for the individuals to stay, so they leave or are removed.

A key relationship is formed that inspires and supports the move.

> "Let us put our heads together and see what life we will make for our children."
>
> –Tatonka Iotanks
> **Chief Sitting Bull of the Lakota**

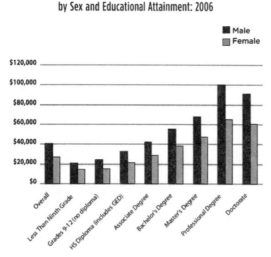

U.S. Median Income for Persons 25 and Older, by Sex and Educational Attainment: 2006

A Little Quiz:

What is the difference in earnings for men and women?

What is the average educational attainment of the group having the most children?

What is the divorce rate?

Who do the children generally live with?

What percentage of individuals ordered to pay child support actually do?

How: Learn as much as you can about yourself,

develop and build your resources,

think about what you want to do, be, and have,

identify talents and skills you have,

understand why it is important to get a formal education,

make a plan that includes getting an education,

use information in this book to understand reasons, rules, and systems,

and learn about your community and what resources are available to you.

Children lead the nation in poverty.
They are the group of people with the largest number living in poverty.
What do leaders do? Leaders drive change. They use the information and knowledge available to lead and choose a better way.

Over the last 30 years the rate of poverty among the elderly has been cut in half.
REALITY: *People over the age of 65 vote more often than any other group of people.*
Register at: www.eac.gov/voter/register.

While people experience many different realities economic and otherwise, it is also true that they share many realities. Consider these common realities:

- All individuals come from a particular part or region of a country.
- All individuals face the possibility of illness or disability.
- All individuals have a heritage and are members of a group based on race.
- All individuals will experience the changes of aging.
- All individuals deal with issues related to their gender.
- All individuals have an economic reality and belong to an economic class.
- All individuals have resources; the amount and how they are used will vary depending on the individual.
- All individuals face challenges and use the resources available to them to meet those challenges.
- All individuals are problem solvers.

Key Points to Remember

1) *The R Rules* presents and explores patterns related to resources and economic realities. The work is based on patterns, *and all patterns have exceptions!* Patterns describe things that happen *most of the time,* not every time. A pattern of behavior in chickens is that they lay eggs. To say that *all* chickens lay eggs would be incorrect, and very upsetting to roosters!

!!??!!

Stereotype: *All* high school teachers lecture every day.
Pattern: *Many* high school teachers lecture every day.

2) *The R Rules* are about diversity of resources. They are *not* a study of racial or cultural diversity. Financial realities occur in all races and in all countries. Economic classification and race are not the same. Economic class is related to economics and is always subject to change. Race is related to common descent or bloodlines and remains a lifelong resource.

He was a wealthy Viking. He was a middle class Viking. He was a poor Viking.

3) Financial or economic reality is determined by the amount of resources, including money, that are available to an individual. Failure in school and at work is often due to a lack of resources or incomplete resources. All people face problems and solve them using the resources available.

4) Social classification and economic classification are not the same. Social class is about personality and popularity. Economic class is about economic realities, resources, and how individuals choose to use them.

5) Three classifications—wealth, middle class, and poverty—will be used to discuss different economic realities and refer to patterns that occur after two generations in one class. All economic classes have unique patterns and challenges. Wealth, middle class, and poverty are relative.

6) Poverty is defined as the extent to which an individual does without resources. Resources include finances, mental, physical, spiritual, support systems, personal strength, and talents and abilities.

7) Mindsets change when individuals have been in the same class for two generations or longer. In *The R Rules,* when economic classes are discussed, we are referring to patterns that occur after people have been in a particular economic class for two generations or more. People who have been in poverty for two generations or more are said to be in *generational poverty. Situational poverty* refers to a change caused by a situation such as a death, loss of a job, or a divorce and is usually shorter in duration. Generational and situational patterns are different.

8) Economic realities can change at any time and are relative to current circumstances, resources, and the environment of the individual.

9) The mental model below shows the patterns used for sorting and decisions making in the three economic classes.

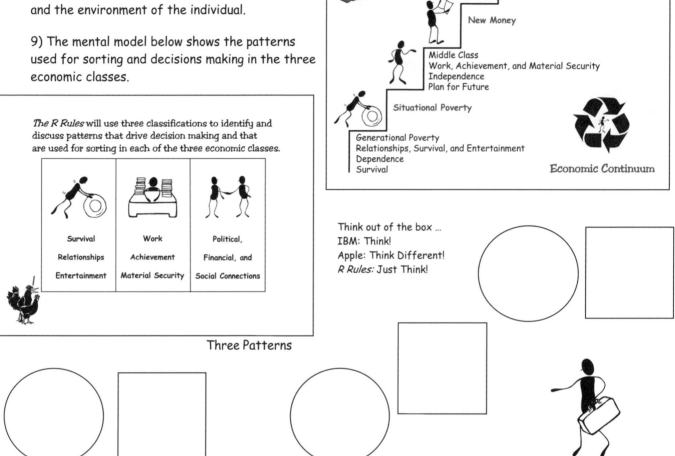

Old Money
Social, Political, and Financial Connections
Interdependence
Legacy

New Money

Middle Class
Work, Achievement, and Material Security
Independence
Plan for Future

Situational Poverty

Generational Poverty
Relationships, Survival, and Entertainment
Dependence
Survival

Economic Continuum

The R Rules will use three classifications to identify and discuss patterns that drive decision making and that are used for sorting in each of the three economic classes.

Survival	Work	Political,
Relationships	Achievement	Financial, and
Entertainment	Material Security	Social Connections

Three Patterns

Think out of the box …
IBM: Think!
Apple: Think Different!
R Rules: Just Think!

10) Individuals bring the behaviors, patterns, and habits of the economic class they grew up in. Because the patterns become rules, set the accepted behaviors, and are often unspoken, we call them hidden rules. They are usually only discovered when you break one. To learn them, individuals need to see and understand patterns or learn them directly from someone they trust.

11) Schools and businesses use the hidden rules of middle class. To succeed at school and work, it is necessary to understand the rules used there.

12) Education and relationships are two things that help individuals move from one economic class to another. Individuals must often change how they spend their time to move from one level of achievement to another.

13) Your mind is a tool, a weapon, and a resource. A tool to invent and discover, a weapon to fight fear and injustice, and a resource to create the world we all want to live in. Understanding patterns and resources will help you identify options and possibilities, choose your own path, and increase your ability to help others do the same.

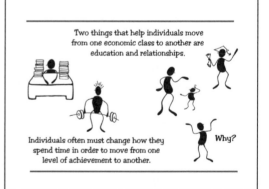

Two things that help individuals move from one economic class to another are education and relationships.

Individuals often must change how they spend time in order to move from one level of achievement to another.

Why?

Reasons, Realities, Patterns, and Mental Models

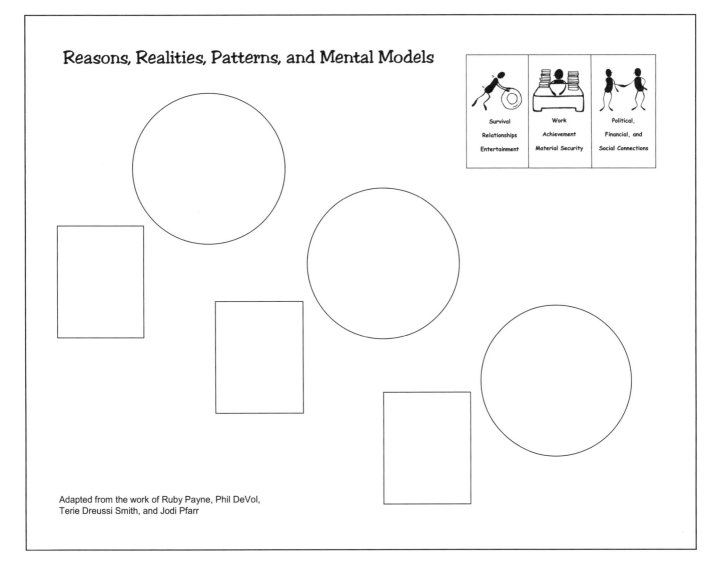

Adapted from the work of Ruby Payne, Phil DeVol,
Terie Dreussi Smith, and Jodi Pfarr

Can an individual live in a reality that is perceived but not actual?
How does having an education make a difference in a person's reality?
Why is it important to give back to your community?

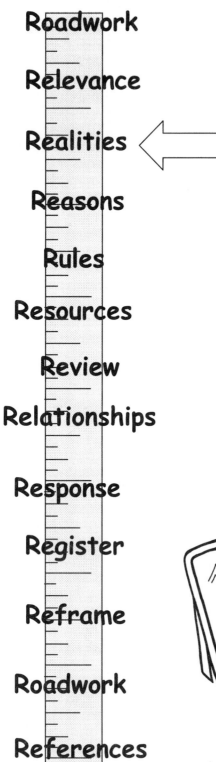

Roadwork

Relevance

Realities ⟵

Reasons

Rules

Resources

Review

Relationships

Response

Register

Reframe

Roadwork

References

What did you learn?

Why is it important?

How can you use what you learned?

Reflection:
What does your current reality look like?

Notes

Chapter 4
REASONS:
The stories we tell ourselves

Ms. Ebert told us we had to bring her an excuse if we missed school. I got really good at writing excuses, but I always wondered why she wanted an excuse instead of the reason.

What they are: A reason is the cause that explains a particular action or event. Reasons are based on perceptions and mental models. Reasons may or may not be obvious and are always subject to personal interpretation. Often patterns have existed for so long that the true reason, root cause, or original meaning is hidden, forgotten, or changed over time.

Why this is important: Until the real reason or root cause is known, efforts to solve a problem, make a change, or improve may not be successful. Reasons are based on information directly related to resources, and because they develop over time, they become accepted patterns of thinking and behaving.

How you can use this information: Use scenarios and tools to determine root cause or actual reasons for situations and behaviors. Consider the stories we tell ourselves and ask what, why, and how. Understanding the real reason something is occurring will help you take control and make changes if they are needed. Here is an example of a process that can be used to uncover reasons or cause and effect.

REASON: the cause, the chain of events, the purpose, the future picture

Five Whys or Why[5]: The Juran Institute published a series of *Quality Minutes* on video in the 1990s. One of them describes a problem with the Jefferson Memorial: The granite was crumbling. What was frustrating to park officials was that none of the other memorials were having this same problem with their granite. So the question was *why?*

Question: *Why* is the granite crumbling on the Jefferson Memorial?
Answer: It is hosed off more than the other memorials.
Question: *Why* is the Jefferson Memorial hosed off more than the other D.C. memorials?
Answer: The Jefferson Memorial has more bird dung.
Question: *Why* does the Jefferson Memorial have more bird dung than the other memorials?
Answer: It has more birds.
Question: *Why* does the Jefferson Memorial have more birds?
Answer: It has more spiders for the birds to eat.
Question: *Why* does the Jefferson Memorial have more spiders than other D.C. memorials?
Answer: It has more flying insects for the spiders to eat.
Question: *Why* does the Jefferson Memorial have more flying insects than other D.C. memorials?
Answer: The lights are turned on too soon at the Jefferson Memorial, thus attracting insects.
Solution: The lights were turned on later and the granite stopped crumbling. By asking *why* enough times, usually at least five, one can find the root causes of problems.

Why?
Why?
Why?
Why?
Why

Draw a mental model for "root cause"

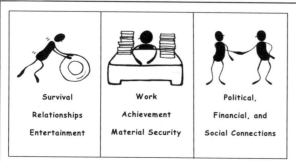

Survival
Relationships
Entertainment

Work
Achievement
Material Security

Political,
Financial, and
Social Connections

Some people ask why.
Some ask why not.
Just ask!

Research

CAUSES OF POVERTY			
Behaviors of the Individual	**Human and Social Capital in the Community**	**Exploitation**	**Political/Economic Structures**
Definition: Research on the choices, behaviors, characteristics, and habits of people in poverty.	*Definition:* Research on the resources available to individuals, communities, and businesses.	*Definition:* Research on how people in poverty are exploited because they are in poverty.	*Definition:* Research on the economic, social, and political, and policy at the international, national, state, and local levels.
Sample topics: Dependence on welfare Morality Crime Single parenthood Breakup of families Intergenerational character traits Work ethic Racism and discrimination Commitment to achievement Spending habits Addiction, mental illness, domestic violence Planning skills Orientation to the future Language experience	*Sample topics:* Intellectual capital Social capital Availability of jobs Availability of well-paying jobs Racism and discrimination Availability and quality of education Adequate skill sets Childcare for working families Decline in neighborhoods Decline in social morality Urbanization Suburbanization of manufacturing Middle-class flight City and regional planning	*Sample topics:* Drug trade Racism and discrimination Payday lenders Sub-prime lenders Lease/purchase outlets Gambling Temp work Sweatshops Sex trade Internet scams	*Sample topics:* Globalization Equity and growth Corporate influence on legislators Declining middle class De-industrialization Job loss Decline of unions Taxation patterns Salary ratio of CEO to line worker Immigration patterns Economic disparity Racism and discrimination

If □ → □ Then

-Philip DeVol, *Facilitator Notes for Getting Ahead in a Just-Gettin'-By World*

Do you see the patterns of cause and effect?

Five reasons that influence economic realities:
- *Educational attainment of the adults in the home*
- *Addiction issues of the adults in the home*
- *Family structure*
- *Immigration*
- *Language issues*

Survival Relationships Entertainment	Work Achievement Material Security	Political, Financial, and Social Connections

Reasons individuals leave one economic reality and move to another:
- *The individual is able to see his or her future.*
- *They know what they want to be, do, or have.*
- *The individual has a specific skill or talent.*
- *A key relationship is formed that inspires or supports the move.*
- *The current reality is too painful; the individual leaves or is removed.*

What, Why, How

What is the reason for or the meaning of these nursery rhymes?

Humpty Dumpty

Jack jump over the candlestick.

Jack and Jill

RING AROUND THE ROSIE
Ring-a-ring o'roses,
A pocket full of posies,
Ashes! Ashes!
We all fall down.

More PATTERNS

Stories, rules, patterns, and understandings develop over time. Often the origin is forgotten and the meanings are changed as they are passed from generation to generation. Stories are a way to pass history from generation to generation. They provide a picture or mental model of events, people, or things that can be used to make a connection to our past or present. Like these nursery rhymes, when individuals from different realities hear stories, they may take on an entirely different meaning.

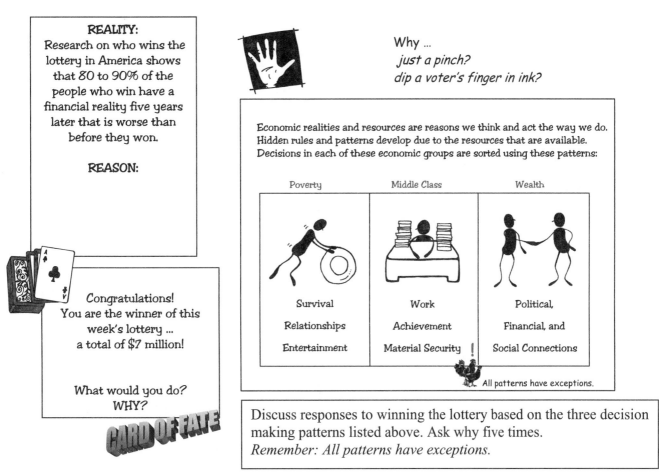

REALITY:
Research on who wins the lottery in America shows that 80 to 90% of the people who win have a financial reality five years later that is worse than before they won.

REASON:

Congratulations!
You are the winner of this week's lottery ...
a total of $7 million!

What would you do?
WHY?

CARD OF FATE

Why ...
just a pinch?
dip a voter's finger in ink?

Economic realities and resources are reasons we think and act the way we do. Hidden rules and patterns develop due to the resources that are available. Decisions in each of these economic groups are sorted using these patterns:

Poverty	Middle Class	Wealth
Survival	Work	Political,
Relationships	Achievement	Financial, and
Entertainment	Material Security	Social Connections

All patterns have exceptions.

Discuss responses to winning the lottery based on the three decision making patterns listed above. Ask why five times.
Remember: All patterns have exceptions.

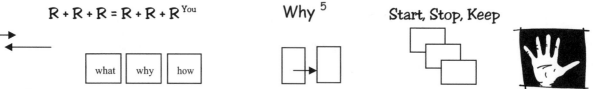

$R + R + R = R + R + R^{You}$ Why ^{5} Start, Stop, Keep

what | why | how

REASONS

Read the behaviors below and think about why they occur based on the resources that are available. In the first box list a reason based on a first look or quick scan. In the second, use patterns, mental models, and your insights to do an MRI—a Multiple Resource Inventory. Then, based on patterns of resources, hidden rules, and connecting to a future picture, write a prescription (Rx) that could be used to build resources.

Are the rules the same everywhere?

At school or work reasons an individual might ...		QUICK SCAN	MRI	Rx
Be disorganized, not be able to find assignments. Have papers stuffed in his/her locker or a messy desk?	1			
Laugh when teacher corrects him/her?	2			
Drop out of school or quit work?	3			
Get very angry when someone asks, "Why did you do that? You should know better!"	4			
Get an assignment back, see a red F on the paper, crumple it up, and throw it in the trash?	5			
Not go to college even though he/she has been awarded a scholarship and has good grades?	6			
Get an assignment back that has a grade of A and stay after school to talk to the teacher about getting an A+?	7			
Physically fight?	8			
Fake not understanding an assignment or make bad grades on purpose?	9			
Use inappropriate language?	10			
Plan everything and write down every assignment, job, and instruction?	11			
Never have school supplies or tools, but often have a new CD or clothing or a nice car?	12			
Be overheard saying, "You are bad, man," to a friend? Or, "You are so ugly ...?"	13			
Talk loudly or entertain during class or meetings?	14			
Not call in when he/she is sick and will not be at school or work.	15			
Not stay after school even though the teacher is willing to tutor and he/she has a failing grade?	16			
Not have work done on a six-week assignment three weeks after the assignment was given?	17			
Not redo or complete an assignment that received a zero?	18			
Not attend a conference or travel to a meeting even though the company is paying for it?	19			

I see, I hear | I tell myself a story | I act

Reasons: the reality
     the stories I tell myself
     the future picture
     the resources
     the hidden rules

The average American changes jobs 8-10 times
and careers 5-6 times in a lifetime.
2003, Curtis and Associates, Inc.

Your mind is a tool, a resource, and a mental weapon.

CARD OF FATE

The
reality
game

Two ears ...
One mouth ...
Listen twice ... talk once.

"It is important to understand
opinions different from your own.

Learn not to be angry, but to set to work understanding
how those opinions came about.

If after you have understood they still seem false,
you can combat them more effectively than if you had
continued to be merely horrified."

-Bertrand Russell

LISTEN = SILENT

What is the current situation?   **You just won the lottery! $7 Million!**

What is the reality of the current situation? _____

_____

Is this important? Why or why not? _____

Do I need to respond? How long can I wait before I respond? How will I respond? _____

_____

 What are possible actions, options, solutions? _____

_____

What resources are available? _____

What resources are missing? _____

Will a different resource work? _____

How can I get this resource? _____

What response will I try? _____

Why ...
will this work? _____

won't it work? _____

How will I know it worked? _____

What else will I try if it doesn't work? Plan B:_____

_____

Roadwork

Relevance

Realities

Reasons ⬅

Rules

Resources

Review

Relationships

Response

Register

Reframe

Roadwork

References

What did you learn?
Why is it important?
How can you use what you learned?

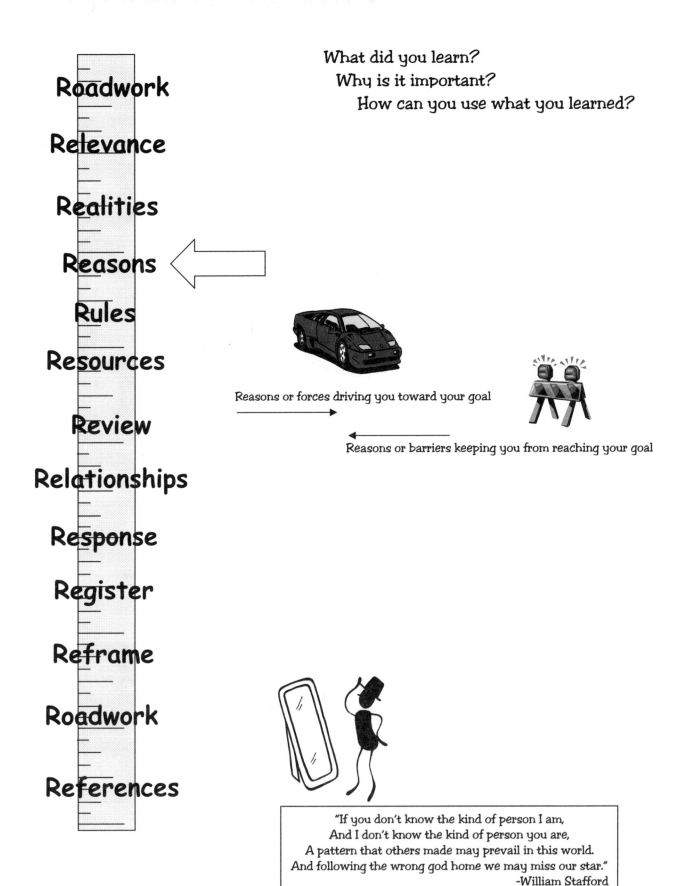

Reasons or forces driving you toward your goal

Reasons or barriers keeping you from reaching your goal

"If you don't know the kind of person I am,
And I don't know the kind of person you are,
A pattern that others made may prevail in this world.
And following the wrong god home we may miss our star."
                                                    -William Stafford

Everyone is a star.
You've just got to find the right constellation.

Notes

Chapter 5
RULES

What they are: Hidden rules are the unspoken, unwritten rules, cues, and habits of a group. Every group of people has a distinct "cueing system" or set of rules that develop over time and become the accepted patterns of behavior. They are customs and traditions—the norm or accepted way things are done. These patterns are often associated with racial and ethnic groups, but are largely unrecognized in economic groups. Rules exist everywhere, and all groups of people and cultures have their own set. Rules provide order and safety and can be formal or informal. The informal rules, the rules that are never published in the handbook, are called "hidden rules." These are the realities and mental models, generally unspoken and unwritten, used to determine how things should be—patterns like who sits in a certain chair at dinner or to watch television, what to wear or not to wear to a job interview, etc. Hidden rules develop over time, are often unnoticed, and become customs, traditions, habits, and the norms of behavior. *The R Rules* discusses the hidden rules and patterns related to three economic classifications. *Remember, all patterns have exceptions.*

Why this is important: Life is like a card game; if you know the patterns and rules, you can decide how you play the game. Likewise, when people know the rules of a group, they can use that information to understand realities and behaviors and make choices. Realities and rules often remain unspoken or hidden; individuals may be unaware they even exist. People use the rules they know and generally assume everyone knows and uses the same set. When an individual breaks a hidden rule, conflicts or judgments can arise. People may think the individual is being rude or is not intelligent. Knowing the rules allows understanding, discussion, choices, and a certain level of emotional comfort.

How you can use this information: Use what you know about hidden rules to choose personal behaviors and understand the behaviors of others. Think of hidden rules as the "rules of this game." Life is like a game; knowing the rules and how and when to play the cards you are dealt can make new situations easier and increase awareness and understanding of others, as well as yourself.

Research shows that the first three minutes of a job interview will determine whether the applicant is suited for the job or not. Often people come from different backgrounds and use different sets of rules. Because the rules are unwritten and often unspoken, the expected set may not be used, and the applicant may be passed over regardless of talents or qualifications.

Peter Senge, in *Schools That Learn,* tells a story about a corporation that opened offices in the Natal region of South Africa. Local tribe members were hired to work as managers. One of the customs of their tribe was to greet each other with specific terms stated in a certain order. The pattern was to say "Sawu bona," meaning "I see you." The expected response was "Skihona," meaning "I am here." This was important because until a person acknowledged they saw you, you did not exist. When other managers, unfamiliar with the pattern, did not follow the practice, it was considered a great disrespect, and misunderstandings occurred. The rules at work and school will almost always be different than the rules at home. Both are resources and must be respected. Choices are based on understanding when and where each set is used.

If you want to see how hidden rules come into play, the next time you answer the phone at work, change the greeting from "Good afternoon" to a greeting you would use with a friend. Park your car in the space that "belongs" to someone else at school or work. Stand up and sing loudly in a library or some other place where the accepted rule is a quiet environment.

Usually rules aren't broken intentionally; they are broken because individuals don't even know they exist. They are hidden. The way you know you broke a hidden rule is by the way others respond, someone gives you *the look,* becomes angry, or things suddenly get very quiet. Sometimes what happened is very clear; other situations may require an explanation from someone who knows the rules and is willing to explain them. Knowing that different sets of rules exist and when to use them will allow you to choose behaviors, develop resources, and better understand the behavior of others. All sets must be respected. *Resources = Choices. The greater the resources, the greater the choices.*

Scripts
Cues
Expectations
Assumptions
Beliefs
Habits
Cultures
Norms

Where do rules come from?

People use the unwritten rules, cues, habits, and understandings of the cultures they grow up in. These rules are unwritten and often unspoken. They are woven through the fabric of everyday life and have been used for so long they are invisible. They influence the way individuals think and use information and are so automatic they become customs, traditions, and habits.

... these rules are called "hidden rules"

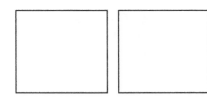

How many times have you held a penny in your hand?

Without looking at the coin, draw the front of a penny in the first box and the back of a penny in the second. Now look at a penny and see how well you did. Hidden rules, like pennies, are everywhere and are often unseen and remain "below the radar."

Actions and beliefs, those things we do automatically and without thinking about them, are habits. Habits control us, or we control them. While habits can develop unconsciously, to change a habit requires a conscious effort and resources.

List below:

Three good habits:	Three bad habits:
_____	_____
_____	_____
_____	_____

Everyday Habits ...
Keys
Wallet
Phone
    Automaticity

What makes a habit good or bad?

A bad habit involves behavior that is destructive or hurtful.
Consider these habits:
- *always blaming others*
- *assuming that others use the same rules or think just like you do*
- *having limited mindsets or the inability to consider other options or possibilities*
- *thinking of yourself as inferior or not as good as others*
- *using negative self-talk*

Behaviors become habits and then realities.

Eleanor Roosevelt said, "No one can make you feel inferior unless you give them license."
A comedian said, "It doesn't really matter what you call me, it matters what I answer to."

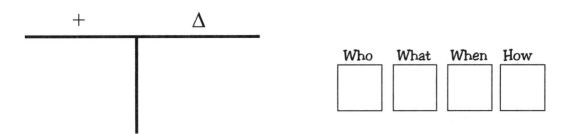

*"We are what we repeatedly do.
Excellence, then, is not an act, but a habit."
—Aristotle*

The chart below is a Plus Delta.

Plus (+) is a symbol for what is working, going well, strengths, or things that should stay the same.

Delta (Δ) is the Greek symbol for change.

On the plus side, list three personal habits that are strengths.

On the delta side, list three personal habits that could be changed or improved.

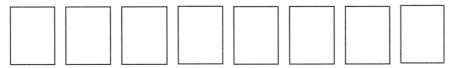

+   Δ

Who	What	When	How

What will you change? *Why* will you change? *How* will you change?

Pick one habit to work on. Will you get rid of a habit or make one better? Remember: *GOOD TO GREAT!*

Changing a habit requires a plan, a conscious effort, and resources.

Use self-talk. *Procedural:* 1. First I will … 2. Then I will … 3. Next I will …

    Positive: "I know I can do this because I am … "

Connect to a future picture: "If I choose to do this, then … "

Research shows that it takes 21 days to make or break a habit.

Check your progress by putting a check and the date in a square every three days.

Plan your work, and then work your plan. If the plan isn't working, rework it.

☐ ☐ ☐ ☐ ☐ ☐ ☐ ☐

Even a blind squirrel finds
an acorn once in a while.
-unknown

*Winners are determined by an event.
Champions require a process.*

Most people are able to win a race one time,
champions win time after time.
Champions and superstars have a process.
They own their habits,
they are in control.
They learn the rules,
they develop their resources.
Most were lucky at least once,
but to keep on winning,
they had to be prepared,
disciplined,
develop abilities,
talents, resources,
know the rules of the game,
and read the patterns.

Write the name of one person you think of as a champion.
Why do you think of them as a champion?
How are you like this person?

Consider the relationships between hidden rules and ...

Habits are those things we do automatically. Habits become patterns and accepted norms of behavior. The group with the most people, money, or power generally determines which behaviors are acceptable.

Assumptions are the information or beliefs that people use without proof that the information is accurate or true. An assumption: *If you are wealthy, you must be smarter than others.*

Expectations are the ways people think things should be or will be. The ways people are expected to be or act. Often expectations are based on past experiences. People expect everyone to know the same hidden rules they do and to use them. If someone does not, they may make an assumption that the person is either rude or not very smart.

Beliefs are what individuals hold to be true about the world using the information they have. Realities are based on how individuals believe the world to be.

Experiences are what we know, have done, and remember.

What do you need to learn?
What do you need to unlearn?

Look at the drawing below. Make up a story about what happened.

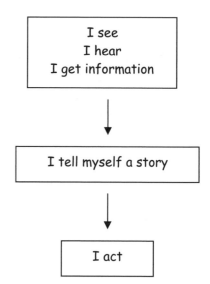

Timothy R. Lucas and Associates
The Fifth Discipline Fieldbook Project –
Schools That Learn

How did your assumptions, expectations, past experiences, and beliefs influence your mindsets and your story?

Culture: the stories we tell ourselves
Mental Models: a mental picture, story, pattern, purpose, structure

Scripts: Computers have operating systems and use scripts. Scripts are a set of directions that are followed in a certain order. Humans have a very sophisticated operating system and also follow scripts. When the computer is switched on, the operating system uses a process that is invisible or hidden from the user to scan every part of the hard drive and load information that is stored there. This information is accessed and used to respond to input. Much like computers, people follow scripts. The mind scans, loads, sorts, and then uses all of the information that has been stored. The information becomes a habit, a mindset, a way of thinking and operating, and is often invisible to the user. Patterns of behavior develop over time. "Fish see water last" is a mental model for patterns that are so automatic they are invisible to the user.

Consider the rules of your family, organization, team, etc. In your home, do family members have certain chairs that only they sit in? Would a visitor find people watching the same television show at the same time every day? Is there a special holiday celebrated in exactly the same way every year? Is it an unwritten rule that family members will be taken care of, no matter what? Until there is a conscious awarenss and disciplined effort to rewrite and use a new script, any information, including all of the habits and mindsets learned growing up, will be loaded and used. These become the mental models or patterns the mind uses to sort information and then act. Individuals bring with them the hidden rules of the class they were raised in and use all of the sets of rules they know to be safe and live well. Even though the environment of the individual may change significantly, many of the patterns of thought, social interaction, cognitive strategies, etc. will remain with and be used by the individual.

There are hidden rules about everything. The way you know you have broken a rule is *the look* people give you when you do. Ruby Payne describes it as "the way you would look at something moving in a wastebasket." There are many hidden rules to examine. The ones discussed here have the greatest impact on learning and success at school and work.

Take these three little quizzes …

HOW ARE YOUR SURVIVAL SKILLS?
from *A Framework for Understanding Poverty*

Could you survive in poverty?

Complete the quiz: Put a check by each item that applies to you.

_____	1.	I know which churches and sections of town have the best garage sales.
_____	2.	I know which thrift stores have name-brand clothing.
_____	3.	I know which grocery stores mark down and which garbage bins can be accessed for food that has been thrown away.
_____	4.	I know how to fight and defend myself physically.
_____	5.	I know how to keep my clothes from being stolen at the Laundromat.
_____	6.	I know how to use the Internet and get a free e-mail account.
_____	7.	I know how to live without a checking account.
_____	8.	I can live without electricity and a phone.
_____	9.	I know how to use a knife as scissors.
_____	10.	I can entertain a group of friends with my personality and my stories.
_____	11.	I know what to do when there isn't money to pay the bills.
_____	12.	I know how to use public transportation and get by without a car.
_____	13.	I know how to get someone out of jail.
_____	14.	I can move in half a day.
_____	15.	I know how to get and use food stamps or an electronic card for benefits.
_____	16.	I know where the free medical clinics are.
_____	17.	I am very good at trading and bartering.
_____	18.	I know how to get a library card.
_____	19.	I know how to use a pawn shop.
_____	20.	I know what to look for in a used car.

Could you survive in middle class?

Complete the quiz: Put a check by each item that applies to you.

_____1.   I know how to register for Little League, soccer, etc.
_____2.   I know the best piano teacher and dance studio.
_____3.   I know which stores are most likely to carry the clothing brands my family wears.
_____4.   I know how to set a table properly.
_____5.   I know how to order in a nice restaurant.
_____6.   I know how to use a credit card, checking account, and savings account.
_____7.   I think about going to college and which colleges I might attend.
_____8.   I know how to apply for a job.
_____9.   I know how to maintain a car and pay for my own gasoline.
_____10.   I know how to get help with my homework and do not hesitate to ask.
_____11.   I know how to decorate the house for the different holidays.
_____12.   I know how to get a library card.
_____13.   I maintain and decorate my room.
_____14.   I know how to use tools and where they are stored.
_____15.   I know how to budget and get a regular allowance.
_____16.   I have access to a computer and the Internet at home.
_____17.   I know the names of our family dentist and doctor.
_____18.   I know which mobile phone plan is the best.
_____19.   I know how to plan a menu and buy food for a week.

Could you survive in wealth?

Complete the quiz: Put a check by each item that applies to you.

_____1.   I can read a menu in English, French, and another language.
_____2.   I have several favorite restaurants in different cities around the world.
_____3.   During the holidays or for special celebrations, I know how to hire a professional to identify the appropriate themes and items with which to decorate the house.
_____4.   I know who I prefer as a trainer, hairstylist, and designer.
_____5.   My family has at least two residences that are staffed and maintained.
_____6.   I know how to treat the members of our domestic staff.
_____7.   I have been to a play in the theater.
_____8.   I fly in our family or company plane.
_____9.   I attend a private school.
_____10.   A member of my family serves on the board of two charities or service organizations.
_____11.   I know the hidden rules of the Junior League.
_____12.   I know the work of several artists and have a favorite art gallery.
_____13.   I know the best private tutors.
_____14.   I know how to keep several social screens between myself and others for protection.
_____15,   I plan to attend the same college my father or other members of our family attended.
_____16.   I understand the terms of my trust.
_____17.   I know the names of our banker and attorney.
_____18.   I do volunteer work for my favorite charity.
_____19.   I know where and how to exchange foreign currency.

FIRST:

If you know most of the answers on the middle class quiz, you might assume that everyone else does too. These are the rules used by school and work. If you did not know many of the items on the quizzes, but knew most of the answers on one, you can understand how individuals make assumptions about the *hidden* rules and resources of others.

NEXT:

It is hoped that completing the quiz increased your understanding of challenges found in all economic classes. Life in any financial reality requires individual strength, intelligence, and the ability to use resources wisely. All people are problem solvers, have resources in varying degrees, and use those resources to meet challenges and live well.

LAST:

In order to move from one class to another successfully, it is necessary to know the rules of the class you are moving to. When individuals grow up in one class and then move to or enter another, they will use the rules of the class they are moving to, but also keep the rules they bring with them. Understanding the rules is important; having resources to know when and how to use them will make all the difference in reaching the future picture you want to live in.

The following examples will help explain parts of the quiz and the chart on the following pages. Use the driving forces that impact decisions in each class to look for these patterns:

	POVERTY	MIDDLE CLASS	WEALTH
DRIVING FORCE →	*Survival, Relationships, Entertainment*	*Work, Achievement, Material Security*	*Financial, Political, and Social Connections*

Walk a mile in my shoes ...
Consider the forces or criteria against which decisions are made in each reality. It is important to understand the hidden rules of different groups without making judgments about whether they are right or wrong. This work is based on patterns; all patterns have exceptions. Resources = Choices.

→

IF the driving force is survival,
 THEN the pattern or rule about food would be: Is there *enough* to eat?
IF the driving force is achievement,
 THEN the pattern or rule about food would be: Is it *good* and *do you like it?*
IF the driving force is about social connections,
 THEN the pattern or rule about food would be: Was it *presented* well? Did it *match the theme* of the party?

The question in the quiz about using a knife as scissors illustrates a pattern: Tools are not always available in poverty. Tools are, in many ways, the identifiers of the middle class, from the kitchen to the garage. The notion of maintaining property and repairing things is dependent upon owning tools and having a place to store them.

Next, consider a student who has an assignment that requires conducting an experiment or building a structure like a backboard. Resources such as scissors, ruler, colored pencils, hammer, saw, or test tubes will be needed. To complete the assignment, these resources will have to be provided.

Being able to physically fight or have someone who is willing to physically defend and protect you is often necessary and valued in poverty. In middle class, being able to use words to negotiate conflict is critical. In wealth, the ability to negotiate and create networks that protect assets is the key. Fists may be used when words and the ability to communicate and negotiate are either unavailable or not respected.

One of the biggest difficulties in achieving financial stability is managing money and having a base of general information about money. It is difficult to manage something you have never had. Money is seen in poverty as an expression of personality and is used for maintaining relationships. The notion of using money for security is truly grounded in the middle and wealthy classes.

One of the biggest differences among classes is the way "the world" is defined. Wealthy individuals view the international scene as their world and may have a favorite restaurant in Brazil or France. Middle class tends to see the world in terms of the national picture, while people in poverty see the world as their neighbors and the immediate area they live in.

Parents in middle class use resources to provide lessons, activities, and experiences to develop a child's talents and capabilities. In wealth, there are expectations about carrying on the family legacy, maintaining networks, and developing new connections. Parents in situational poverty may see college as a way to achieve economic stability. Children in generational poverty may not be encouraged to go away to college because there is a fear that the children may not come back home. When a parent needs a child to stay with a brother or sister, after-school tutoring or other activities will be less important than the family.

In middle class, *things* are possessions. In wealth, one-of-a-kind objects are highly prized possessions. In poverty, *things* have often been sold in order to survive, and the most valuable "possessions" are the relationships and people you have in your life.

In wealth, to be introduced or accepted, one must have an individual who is already accepted by the group make the introduction. To stand back and not introduce yourself in a middle class setting is not the norm and might be considered rude. In poverty, it is not unusual for a comment about personality or style to be made about an individual as he or she is being introduced.

In poverty, resources are limited, so several people may live in a very small space. Usually there are several conversations taking place at once; the television and/or stereo may also be turned on. Dwellings are situated close together, and noise from the neighbors and traffic may be heard. Schedules are often not traditional. People may work more than one job, so people come and go at different times. In wealth and middle class, resources are used to purchase space. Houses are set apart and there are several rooms and fewer people sharing the space. Schedules are more traditional, allowing more time for study and leisure.

Individuals may know and use the hidden rules from any or all of the economic groups, or may only know and use the hidden rules of the one in which they were raised. Understanding what the hidden rules are, why they are used, and how and where to use different rules is comparable to being a gifted athlete who plays football, basketball, and hockey, or a musician able to play several different muscial instruments. School, work, and home are like different events or games. Different rules are used—one set for school, one set for work, another set for home. All are valuable and must be respected. Schools and work use the rules of middle class. The rules used at school and work are not better than those used at home, they are just different. Life is like a card game. You can't control the cards you are dealt, but if you know the rules and can see the patterns, you can decide how to play and win more often.

Use a WWH tool for further study.
WHAT: First, make sure you understand the rule.
WHY: Next, use the driving forces and ask why the hidden rule exists, is important, or makes sense.
HOW: Find additional examples of how the rule would look if it was used or observed in daily life.

	POVERTY	MIDDLE CLASS	WEALTH
DRIVING FORCES →	*Survival, Relationships, Entertainment*	*Work, Achievement, Material Security*	*Financial, Political, and Social Connections*
Time	Present most important. Decisions made based on immediate survival and feelings.	Future most important. Decisions made against future ramifications.	Traditions and history most important. Decisions partially based on tradition and decorum.
Money	To be used, spent.	To be managed.	To be conserved, invested.
Power	Linked to respect. People respond to personal power, ability to defend, protect. Power relative to resources available.	Power is separate from respect. People respond to positional power, ability to negotiate. Power is linked to taking responsibility for solutions. Power in institutions run by middle class.	People respond to expertise, must have influence and connections. Power is linked to information. People in wealth set direction for business, corporations, and public policy.
Examples			
Personality	Is for entertaining. Sense of humor highly valued.	Is for acquisition and stability. Achievement is highly valued.	Is for connections. Financial, political, and social connections are highly valued.
Social Emphasis	Social inclusion of people he/she likes.	Emphasis is on self-governance and self-sufficiency.	Emphasis is on social exclusion.
Acceptance/Love	Acceptance conditional, based on whether the individual is liked.	Acceptance conditional, based largely on achievement.	Acceptance conditional, related to social standing and connections.
Humor	About people.	About situations.	About social faux pas.
Examples			
Food	Key question: Did you get enough? Quantity important.	Key question: Did you like it? Quality important.	Key question: Was it presented well? Presentation important.
Clothing	Clothing valued for its individual style and expression of personality.	Clothing valued for its quality and acceptance into norm of middle class. Label important.	Clothing valued for its artistic sense and expression. Designer important.
Possessions	Relationships with people.	Things.	One-of-a-kind objects, legacies, pedigrees.
Family Structure	Tends to be matriarchal.	Tends to be patriarchal.	Depends on who has the money.
Examples			
Destiny	Believes in fate. Cannot do much to mitigate circumstances.	Believes in choice. Can control the future with good choices now.	Noblesse oblige.
Worldview	Sees world in terms of local setting.	Sees world in terms of national setting.	Sees world in terms of international setting.
Language	Casual register. Language is about survival.	Formal register. Language is for negotiation.	Formal register. Language is about networking.
Education	Valued and revered as abstract, but not a reality.	Crucial for climbing success ladder and making money.	Necessary tradition for making and maintaining connections.
Parenting	Development of resources to live in a changing environment.	Developing talents and providing experiences.	Carrying on legacies, new connections, noblesse oblige.
Examples			

HIDDEN RULES

The discussion and examples could continue about hidden rules. The key point is that whether or not a person knows the hidden rules determines so much of our initial impression of that individual and his/her capabilities. Individuals use the rules they grew up with. People have expectations and beliefs about how things should be and how people should act. People make assumptions. There is an assumption that if individuals do not know the rules, they must not be intelligent or they are being rude. Knowledge of these hidden rules, or lack of it, is often the factor that keeps an individual from getting a job, passing a test, having the ability to choose behaviors, or winning a game. When individuals understand the rules they can see options, understand behaviors, and make choices. It is important to honor individual choices and not make judgments based on the set of rules others choose. Understanding the rules does not mean an individual will choose to use them; it simply means there is a choice. Resources = Choices.

Rules

Sawu bona.
Sikhona.

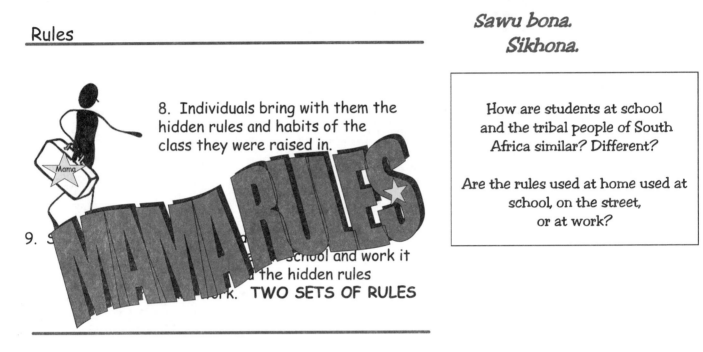

8. Individuals bring with them the hidden rules and habits of the class they were raised in.

9. S̶̶ ̶ ̶ ̶ ̶school and work it ̶ ̶ ̶ the hidden rules ̶ ̶k. **TWO SETS OF RULES**

How are students at school and the tribal people of South Africa similar? Different?

Are the rules used at home used at school, on the street, or at work?

Rules + Rigor + Relationships = Resources + Results + Respect
If there are different sets of rules, what do you need to remember?

- They are "hidden," often unspoken and unwritten.
- One set of rules is not better than any other, they are simply different.
- All sets of rules must be respected.
- Know when and why to use each set of rules.
- Use the rules to understand and improve yourself, not to judge or manipulate others.
- You learn the rules by getting an education and having someone you trust explain the rules in a relationship of mutual respect.
- Individuals bring with them the set of rules they were raised with.
- Individuals can use all of the rules they know, not just one set.
- Use the rules to be in control, to be respected, to keep from being cheated, and to win in the game of life.
- Knowing the rules is a resource. Resources = Choices.

Watch for hidden rules in movies and books.

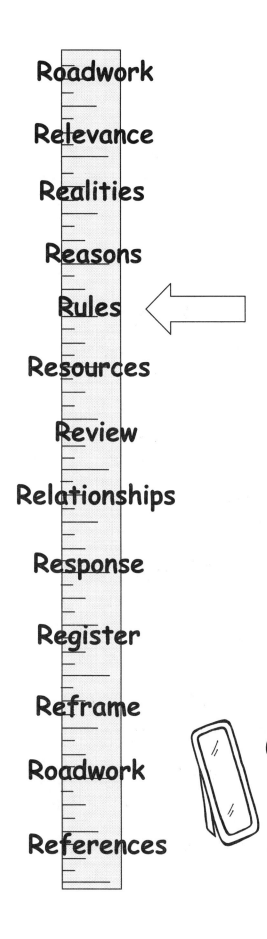

Roadwork

Relevance

Realities

Reasons

Rules

Resources

Review

Relationships

Response

Register

Reframe

Roadwork

References

What did you learn?
Why is it important?
How will you use this information?

A Little Quiz About *Hidden Rules of Class at Work*

from *Hidden Rules of Class at Work* by Ruby Payne and Don Krabill

Complete the quiz: Put a check by each item that applies to you.

Could you survive in an unskilled labor position?

_____1.　I know how to fight and can physically hold my own.
_____2.　I will quit on the spot if the boss makes me mad.
_____3.　I can go without work for long periods of time and still survive.
_____4.　I know how to file for unemployment.
_____5.　I use the sentence, "I was looking for a job when I found this one."
_____6.　I often have to make personal phone calls at work.
_____7.　I know how to live without a checking account.
_____8.　I know how to ask for an advance on my paycheck.
_____9.　I often use casual register at work.
_____10.　I openly discuss disagreements with my boss and flaws I see in my boss.

Could you survive in beginning supervision?

(Hourly wage, responsibility for the group with no say on hire/fire.)

_____1.　I can work side by side with the crew to get the job done without losing my authority.
_____2.　I know how to stay out of the discussion while everyone else is complaining about the boss.
_____3.　I can anticipate what the boss will want or what is needed to complete the job.
_____4.　I can respond to written reports in writing.
_____5.　I can settle most disagreements without going to the boss.
_____6.　I am able to determine what is important and what is not important to report to the boss.
_____7.　I can teach newly hired workers to do their tasks.
_____8.　I know how to do my job and avoid getting caught up in the work of others.
_____9.　I can deal with the "you are one of them" comments from the group I supervise.
_____10.　I understand the importance of confidential information remaining confidential.

Could you survive in mid-management? (Salary, duties, and supervisory responsiblities.)

_____1.　I know how to sort through paperwork and determine and address priorities.
_____2.　I know which volunteer efforts are most important to the company.
_____3.　I understand the difference between the written goals and the real goals of the company.
_____4.　I know how to manage the politics of administrative structure in order to meet goals.
_____5.　I know which administrative assistants and bosses contol the informal power structure.
_____6.　I participate in professional development and training programs.
_____7.　I use and understand different registers of language.
_____8　I use a planner or time management system.
_____9.　I know the patterns of promotion and the corporate structure in the company.
_____10.　If I have personal problems, I don't discuss them openly at work.
_____11.　I know which subjects cannot be discussed openly at meetings.

Could you survive in a corporate executive position?

(Salary, bonus, stock options, accountable to board of directors.)

_____1. I know how to negotiate a contract with the appropriate perks for my position.

_____2. I use corporate residences when I travel and travel first class or by corporate jet.

_____3. My spouse understands how important his/her role is to my prospects for promotion.

_____4. I participate in one of these sports: golf, tennis, sailing, or a sport/activity where high levels of resources are required in order to participate.

_____5. I know the best restaurants, clubs, and locations in several cities around the world.

_____6. When traveling, I have favorite hotels in which I know the concierge, who advises me on the best entertainment, clubs, and restaurants.

_____7. I can get last-minute tickets to football bowl games, the World Series, etc.

_____8. I can select the best wines by year and maker.

_____9. I can read a corporate financial statement, see omissions, and figure the worth of a company on the spot.

_____10. I understand how important my political, financial, and social connections are to the wellbeing of the corporation, and I work to keep and develop them.

_____11. I know how to deveop and protect my corporate turf.

_____12. I speak several languages and know which register is appropriate for the situation.

_____13. I know which charities and political causes the corporation supports.

_____14. I have collegial relationships with several of the members of the board of directors.

_____15. I know how to avoid participating in the bribery systems of other countries.

_____16. I know how to secure and protect personal and corporate data.

_____17. I know how to present our corporate information so our corporation is seen in the best light.

Could you survive as a self-made millionaire? (First generation wealth.)

_____1. I have a high energy level.

_____2. I have the ability to make connections.

_____3. I can delegate.

_____4. I have an innate, gut sense about people and/or ideas.

_____5. I can multitask—manage several tasks or projects simultaneously.

_____6. I can prioritize my time.

_____7. I can give up relationships for a period of time to move effectively in the company.

_____8. I identify and use the tools of analytical measurement that track company progress, particularly during periods of fast growth. (Percentages versus numbers.)

_____9. I can live for long periods of time with financial uncertainty, lack of recognition, and lack of sleep.

What resources will you develop?

Why?

How?

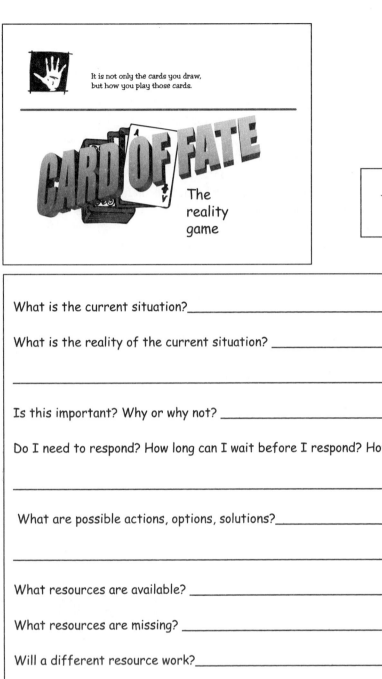

It is not only the cards you draw, but how you play those cards.

CARD OF FATE

The reality game

You just received a phone call. You have an interview this Friday at 10 a.m. for a job you really want.

What is the current situation?_____

What is the reality of the current situation? _____

_____

Is this important? Why or why not? _____

Do I need to respond? How long can I wait before I respond? How will I respond? _____

_____

What are possible actions, options, solutions?_____

_____

What resources are available? _____

What resources are missing? _____

Will a different resource work?_____

How can I get this resource? _____

What response will I try?_____

Why will this work?_____

Why won't it work? _____

How will I know it worked? _____

What else will I try if it doesn't work? Plan B: _____

_____

Resources for Interviews

Practice answering questions that may be asked during the interview:

1. Tell me about yourself.
2. Why are you interested in this job/position?
3. What are your qualifications for this job?
4. How will your past jobs/experiences be of benefit if you are hired for this job?
5. What are your strengths? What are your weaknesses? (Discuss ways to answer these.)
6. What are your career goals?
7. What is your work style? For example, do you prefer to work alone or with a team?
8. How much do you expect as a salary for this position?
9. Why should we hire you?
10. What makes you the best candidate for this job?
11. Do you have any questions you would like to ask us?
12. How would you describe yourself?
13. What else would you like us to know that we have not asked?

Dress: Identify basic interview wardrobe; fairly conservative and appropriate for the field you will be interviewing in. Consider type of job, location, duties, and hidden rules.
We recommend a white blouse/shirt and dark skirt/slacks. The fit of the clothing is important.
Use this form for the practice interviewer to complete and provide you with feedback.
Shirt/Blouse:_____ Pants/Skirt:_____Shoes:_____
Overall Appearance:_____

Language: Formal register and language of vocation; nonverbal communication: body language, eyes, tone of voice. Manners: please, thank you, Mr., Ms., handshake; avoid negative comments about past employers.

Preparation: Job application completed; personal resume, two copies; information about the company, the company's purpose and policies. Business card. Resume in folders and presented to interviewer.

Practice: with a business person, parent, peer, or partner outside of or during class.

Interview Rubric (develop as a class if possible): Completed by interviewers and provided to students after interview. Consider how questions were answered, how prepared the student was, information about the job, interest, and general presentation.

1. Applicant was properly dressed.	1 2 3 4 5
2. Applicant shook hands.	1 2 3 4 5
3. Applicant brought resume.	1 2 3 4 5
4. Applicant used formal register.	1 2 3 4 5
5. Applicant spoke clearly and answered questions concisely.	1 2 3 4 5
6. Applicant used proper body language, maintained eye contact.	1 2 3 4 5
7. Applicant exhibited self-confidence.	1 2 3 4 5
8. Applicant was enthusiastic and ready to begin work.	1 2 3 4 5

Self-Evaluation: *Evaluate yourself prior to reviewing any feedback from others.*
What do you think you did well during the interview?
What do you need to improve or practice?
What did you learn about yourself, and what did you learn about an interview?
Would you hire yourself on the basis of your interview? Use a why, what, and how process.

Adapted from the work of Teri Owen and Christine Sterton

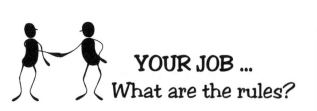

YOUR JOB ...
What are the rules?

Why ...

Workers who understand the rules
and have resources have choices,
get health benefits, retirement funds,
promotions, and are respected.

How...

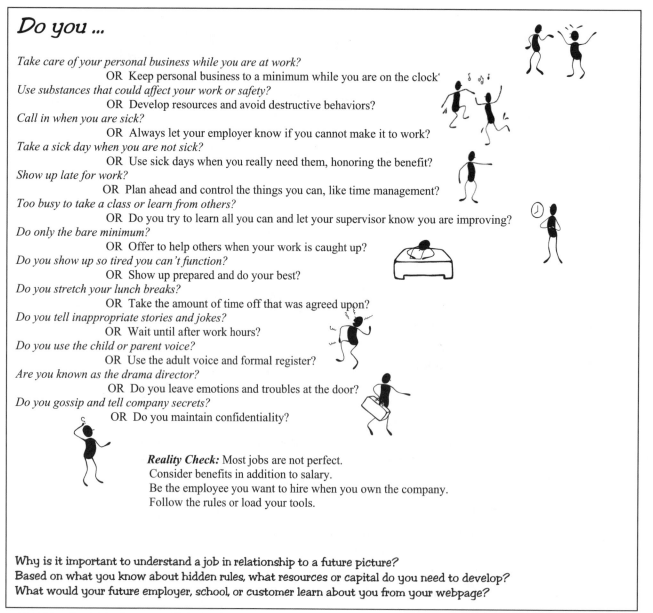

✓ Yourself...

Language
Integrity
Emotional Strength
Support System
Mental Abilities
Knowledge of Hidden Rules
Purpose
Financial Management
Picture of the Future
Physical Appearance
Time Management
Persistence and Perseverance
Relationship Management
Ability to Self-Govern

Do you ...

Take care of your personal business while you are at work?
        OR Keep personal business to a minimum while you are on the clock'
Use substances that could affect your work or safety?
        OR Develop resources and avoid destructive behaviors?
Call in when you are sick?
        OR Always let your employer know if you cannot make it to work?
Take a sick day when you are not sick?
        OR Use sick days when you really need them, honoring the benefit?
Show up late for work?
        OR Plan ahead and control the things you can, like time management?
Too busy to take a class or learn from others?
        OR Do you try to learn all you can and let your supervisor know you are improving?
Do only the bare minimum?
        OR Offer to help others when your work is caught up?
Do you show up so tired you can't function?
        OR Show up prepared and do your best?
Do you stretch your lunch breaks?
        OR Take the amount of time off that was agreed upon?
Do you tell inappropriate stories and jokes?
        OR Wait until after work hours?
Do you use the child or parent voice?
        OR Use the adult voice and formal register?
Are you known as the drama director?
         OR Do you leave emotions and troubles at the door?
Do you gossip and tell company secrets?
         OR Do you maintain confidentiality?

Reality Check: Most jobs are not perfect.
Consider benefits in addition to salary.
Be the employee you want to hire when you own the company.
Follow the rules or load your tools.

Why is it important to understand a job in relationship to a future picture?
Based on what you know about hidden rules, what resources or capital do you need to develop?
What would your future employer, school, or customer learn about you from your webpage?

Adapted from New Mexico Department of Labor brochure

Notes

Chapter 6
RESOURCES

What they are: A resource is anything available to a person that can be used to support or help. *The R Rules* will identify and explore eight basic resources that are vital to success and living well. These eight are: financial, emotional, mental, spiritual, physical, support systems, relationships and role models, and knowledge of hidden rules. Other important resources such as language will also be discussed, but these eight are considered basic and serve as the foundation for all of the others.

Why this is important: Generally, success is thought of only in terms of financial resources. While finances are important, they are not the only difference or reason people are able to succeed. An individual's ability to use the resources available is as important as the amount of resources that are available.

Poverty is defined as extent to which an individual does without resources. The more resources an individual has access to, the more choices that person has. Resources are interconnected, and each one influences the others. An example would be a billionaire who can't add, subtract, or read. While financial resources are high, the resources to keep and manage those financial resources are low. To avoid being cheated and making poor choices, and to understand systems, resources must be developed or purchased. Support systems like accountants, lawyers, investment counselors, and financial advisors may be hired, but without mental resources there is still a risk of being cheated. Without emotional resources relationships, decisions, and responses will influence how financial resources are used. The more resources individuals have, the easier it is to be in control, make changes, respond to situations, and get desired results.

How you can use this information: Learn about the eight basic resources, complete an inventory of your personal resources, then use strategies and information to create a plan to increase and use them to get what you want. Use case studies to learn and discuss how resources relate to daily life, decisions, and options. Work as a group to develop a list of resources that can be accessed and used by youth in your area, then publish and distribute the list. Any time you make a plan, consider what resources are available, what resources will be needed, and what resources can be developed or substituted for those that are missing. Everyone has a different set of resources that can be used as a foundation to develop and increase others.

Always consider resources when planning, responding, or giving advice.

In order to increase the books and reading materials available to her students, a teacher decided all of her students should have their own public library cards. The assumption was that students did not go to the library because they didn't have library cards. In reality many of the students already had library cards but did not go to the library because they didn't have transportation to and from the library or they owed late fees. Resources are interconnected, and success is often determined by one or two resources that are foundational to the others. Consider "hidden rules" and realities different from your own. David had resources to earn a college scholarship but needed assistance understanding and navigating the system in order to use them. Resources are interconnected, and when one resource is missing it can make the others difficult or impossible to use.

On a farm in rural New Mexico a man and his wife shared a dream. They dreamed that each one of their five children would have a college degree. The family had very limited financial resources, but working together they were able to support each child as they made their dream a reality. Each of the children wanted to attend college and each shared a common concern—the sadness of leaving their friends and family. A plan developed, and all of the children decided they would attend the same college.

Every week family members loaded one of two red coolers with fresh milk, eggs, butter, and depending on the season, anything else that the farm had to offer. When the ten o'clock bus arrived in the college town, 200 miles from the family farm, the cooler full of food was picked up and the empty cooler sent home. The cycle continued week after week for many years until all of the children had graduated.

Knowing how to access and use resources is as important as having them. Life is like a card game; you get good hands and bad hands. Knowing the rules and how to play are keys to winning. Money is one resource. Read further to learn about others.

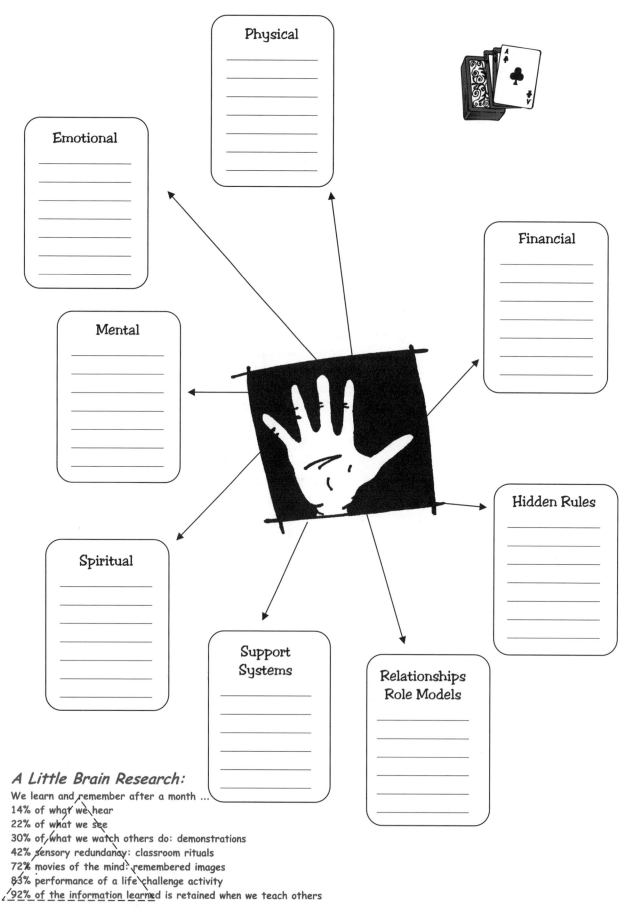

Physical

Emotional

Financial

Mental

Hidden Rules

Spiritual

Support Systems

Relationships Role Models

A Little Brain Research:

We learn and remember after a month ...

14% of what we hear
22% of what we see
30% of what we watch others do: demonstrations
42% sensory redundancy: classroom rituals
72% movies of the mind: remembered images
83% performance of a life challenge activity
92% of the information learned is retained when we teach others

–Dr. G. Phillips, National School Improvement Project

RESOURCES
Use this form to review and check resources.

What is capital?
What is social capital?
What is intellectual capital?
What is bonding capital?
What is bridging capital?

1. Financial
Having the money to purchase goods and services.
Money can be used to purchase resources.

2. Physical
Having physical health and mobility—the ability to walk, move around, and care for yourself without help.

3. Emotional
Being able to choose and control emotional responses, particularly to negative situations, without engaging in destructive behavior to yourself or others. This is an internal resource and shows itself through stamina, perseverance, use of resources and choices.
Doing the right thing when the going is tough and you are alone.

4. Mental
Having the mental abilities and acquired skills (reading, writing, and computing) to deal with daily life.

5. Spiritual
Believing in purpose, power greater than self, and future; a source of personal strength, mission, and hope.

6. Support Systems
Having friends, family, and backup resources available and willing to help in times of need.
These are external resources. Who and/or what can you count on when assistance is needed that won't ask you to engage in destructive behavior?

7. Relationships/Role Models
Having frequent access to individuals who are appropriate, who care, and who do not engage in self-destructive behavior or ask you to. The resource money cannot buy: relationships of mutual respect.

8. Knowledge of Hidden Rules
Knowing the unspoken cues and habits of a group or groups; which hidden rules are used, when, and where.

9. Language and Voice
The ability to use five registers, syntax, structure, and voice appropriately to communicate and negotiate.

Rate your personal resources each month. Use a scale of zero to six. Zero is the lowest, six is the highest.
Use the information to see patterns, causes, predict, and plan. Use and develop resources to increase choices.

Month	9	10	11	12	1	2	3	4	5	6	7	8	9
Financial													
Physical													
Emotional													
Mental													
Spiritual													
Support Systems													
Role Models													
Relationships Mutual Respect													
Hidden Rules													
Language and Voice													

Goal: To develop resources that will allow me to be ...

    independent
    in control and able to respond to various situations
    respected and a role model for others
    aware of hidden rules and understand and choose appropriate behaviors
    able to have and maintain relationships of mutual respect
    a person with a future picture and hope
    and ...

more resources = more choices

Scenarios

On the following pages you will find scenarios about several different people. Scenarios are skeletons of stories, simply the facts or realities. Many of the details have been have been left out in order to see and focus on resources. After you read each scenario, use the form below to record what resources are available. If the resource is available, place a Y in the box. If the resource is not available, place an N in the box. If you are uncertain or information is not provided in the scenario, place a ? in the box.

Resource Analysis

Name	Financial	Emotional	Mental	Spiritual	Physical	Support Systems	Hidden Rules	Relationships Role Models
Opie								
Oprah								
Shawnise								
Habib								
Kate								
Geraldo								
Emerson								
Eileen Wisteria								
Luke								

Opie and Oprah

Background

Opie is a 12-year-old African American girl and the oldest of five children. She runs the household because her mother, Oprah, works long hours as a domestic. Grandmother, who is 80 is senile, lives with them, as does an out-of-work uncle.

You are Opie's mother, Oprah. You are a 32-year-old black female. You were married for ten years to your husband; he was killed in a car accident on his way to work two years ago. You work long hours for a doctor and his family as a domestic. You go to the Missionary Baptist Church every Sunday, where you lead the choir. Your employer treats you well and you take home about $300 every week. You ride public transportation to work and the church bus on Sunday. You want your children to go to college even though you did not finish high school.

Current Situation

Your employer gives you a $400 Christmas bonus. You thank the Lord at church for the gift. After church, three different people approach you privately. One asks for $50 to have the electricity turned on; one asks you for $100 to feed her brother's family; one asks for $60 to replace a broken pair of glasses. You were hoping to save some money for an emergency.

Opie has the opportunity to be in a state-sponsored competition that requires after-school practices. You want her to do that, but must have her home after school every day.

What resources do Opie and Oprah have?

Shawnise

Background

You are in the tenth grade and are a white female, 16 years old. You barely made it to school on time today because you had to get your eight brothers and sisters ready for school. Your mother didn't come home last night and you aren't sure where she is. You just hope and pray you get to the mailbox before she does when the welfare check comes in. Two weeks ago you called the school and told them you were sick so you could stay home and get the mail. Then you lied to your mother and said that the check hadn't come, because there was no food in the house and you couldn't let your brothers and sisters starve.

Your grades are B's and C's and you feel happy about that. You could get straight A's if you had time to do your projects. You ace most of the tests, but you don't have time to do the homework. One of the teachers last week told you that you were bright but lazy. You didn't say anything. How could you explain? The only things in your life that matter are your bothers and sisters, who have five different fathers.

You can't remember a time that you didn't take care of them. You remember when you used to steal from people that you babysat for because your mother told you to. But it just made you feel bad, so you refused to steal, even when it meant you had to go hungry. You can't remember a time when you haven't been hungry sometime during the week.

You want to be a teacher. You remember your fifth-grade teacher, who brought you a meal on Thanksgiving. You were grateful because there was no food in the house. You believe that if you were a teacher you could help kids too.

Current Situation

The teacher is lecturing on the civilization of Greece, and while you are interested, you are wondering what is happening at home. You left your 4-year-old brother at home alone today because your mother wasn't home and you can't miss any more school this six weeks. He has stayed at home alone before.

Last night Sally cried because she didn't have three dollars to go on the field trip. Johnny cried because he couldn't go to a birthday party. You don't have a car. The girls in P.E. laughed at you today because you are fat. You know that fat might keep you alive, and you have to eat when the food is there. The girls in class right now are passing notes about their dates. You just want to make sure your 4-year-old brother is OK.

What are Shawnise's resources?

Habib

Background

You are an African American male, age 18. The reason you come to school is because it is a condition of your probation. You are not really a bad person. It just seems that you are always at the wrong place at the wrong time. You don't have a malicious bone in your body; you are likeable and easily persuaded. Your one great attribute is that you are one heck of a fighter. The women like you. You played on the football team, but just couldn't keep up the grades. Besides, women were much more fun than football.

You went on probation when you were 16. You and your friends were looking for something to do, so you broke into the local pawnshop. It was one of those days that was just no good. You came home from school and found your mother beaten up by her latest boyfriend. Shirley, your younger sister, took her two babies and left. You called an ambulance for your mother but didn't go to the hospital. She missed a couple days of work because of the beating. You were so mad you went looking for the boyfriend. You and your girlfriend had a fight. Breaking into the pawnshop sounded like a good idea at the time. But you got caught and were charged with armed robbery. Juan had loaned you his gun and you had put it in your pocket.

You would like to help with the money, but you can't get a job because of your arrest and the fact that you are on probation for armed robbery.

Current Situation

You attend alternative school. You can read fairy well. You like people and enjoy being with them. But in your heart you are scared for your younger brother. As you wrote to the teacher one day, "I want my little brother to be successful in life. I want him to be the best he can be in whatever he wants to do. But I know I don't want him to hang in the streets 'cause the streets aren't gonna lead to a good life for him. I know from experience 'cause I rapped up in the streets and it ain't cool. All the cool ones are dead. It's all based on money. Money runs the system so I'm gonna make sure I have plenty of that."

What are Habib's resources?

Kate

Background

You are a 16-year-old white female two months away from high school graduation. You would like to go to college someday, and you make good grades. There is no money for college, but the school counselor gave you information about a business school and about joining the Army. You are an only child and live with your mother. Your parents divorced when you were 11, and you have worked since you were 12 to help your mother pay the bills. Your father lives in across town but has not spoken to you since you got into a fight with this wife. Your apartment is small, but it works out since your mother is gone most of the time. She has a new boyfriend and things seem serious. You hate the mess she and her friends make when they show up at your apartment. You found out your best friend is no longer allowed to come to your house, but that is OK because you are embarrassed that her house is so different from yours.

Current Situation

Your mother told you today before you left for school that she and her boyfriend are leaving town. She called her boss, quit her job, and said you would pick up her equipment later in the week. You told her goodbye and went to school because you had a final. When you got home your mother and the furniture were gone, but she left your dog.

It has been three weeks and you have not heard from your mother. The rent is due, and you don't have enough to pay the rent and the utilities. You went to the bank and found out your joint checking account had been closed. When you get your paycheck next week, there won't be enough money to pay the rent even if you don't buy food.

What are Kate's resources?

Geraldo

Background

You are a Hispanic male, 13 years old, and you are in the seventh grade. You are a gang member. It's a matter of pride. When you were 11 you watched your cousin die after he was shot by a rival gang.

Your mother attends mass every Saturday, and you love her. You know the rules of the house. However, the rules of the street are different. Last week your gang made $4,000 selling drugs. This money was split between ten gang members.

Current Situation

Today is the anniversary of your cousin's death. You took a little acid before you went to school because it seemed like the only way to get through. You really like your reading teacher, but all you could do was giggle. It beats crying. You haven't turned in your assignments for the last two weeks. But you could do almost all of them with one hand tied behind your back if you felt like it.

You are watching your back. Today one of the police officers at the school assembly was watching you and you watched him. Rumor has it that there will be a fight between your gang and a rival gang soon.

Today you watched Tony at lunch. Tony's dad drives a Mercedes and drops him off every morning at school. You wonder what it would be like to have money and not worry about dying. There isn't any reason to do well in school; you will be dead before you are 25. You might as well enjoy life.

Like you wrote in your journal in Reading, "I would like adults to know that people my age are different than when they came up. They grew up different than I did. I grew up with sex, money, murder, and banging in the streets. Besides, they want me to do what they want. Well, what they want at home is easy, but as soon as I leave those four walls of home sweet home comes the hard life. As soon as I'm in those streets, it turns into a nightmare. It makes me want to get away from the violence. That is why I have no one, because *faithful* is not in my vocabulary. I'm only faithful to them streets."

What are Geraldo's resources?

Emerson
Background

You are a 17-year-old Native American male, a senior in high school. For as long as you can remember your father has been a mean drunk. But you haven't been home since you were 14, when he kicked you out. Your mother cried and cried, but then he beat her into silence.

You remember the night you were kicked out. You had no place to go, so you slept on the church steps because you believed you would be safe there. You rummaged food from the garbage bins of fast food places and restaurants. You kept going to school because at least you were safe there. You got a job at a restaurant even though you were underage and got a cheap apartment a couple of months later.

Current Situation

At 16 you got a full-time job working evenings for minimum wage. There's a counselor at school who keeps track of you and how you are doing in school. This week he came with a stack of math homework that you need to do. Your brother is living with you now. You have told the counselor that you think you will just quit. You are so discouraged, and the math teacher told you in front of the class yesterday that anyone who is a senior and still in Algebra I might as well drop out of school.

But the counselor told you he was counting on you. He knew it was rough, but he knew you could do it. So you agreed to do the homework for the counselor. God knows you hate the algebra teacher. The counselor told you to come by at 7 in the morning and he would help you.

There are no girls in your life. All you have time for is to go to work, go to school, and sleep.

What are Emerson's resources?

Eileen and Wisteria
Background

Eileen is a 10-year-old white girl who lives with her 70-year-old grandmother, Wisteria, who is on Social Security. Eileen doesn't know who her father is. Her mother has been arrested four times for prostitution and/or drug possession in the last two years. About once a month Mother sobers up and wants Eileen back as her child.

You are Eileen's grandmother, Wisteria. You get about $150 a week from Social Security. Your daughter, Eileen's mother, has been in trouble for years, and while you have given up on her, you couldn't stand to see Eileen in a foster home, so you have taken her into your home. Eileen's mother is in and out of jail, and one of her pimps usually gets her out. The last time she came to see Eileen, Eileen cried and cried after she left and said she never wanted to see her mother again. You have a little money in savings but don't want to use it yet. Your house and car are paid for. You worry what will happen to Eileen if you get sick and die, and you pray each day you can make it until Eileen is 18. You don't see as well as you once did. All of your relatives are dead or distant. Every Sunday you and Eileen go to the United Methodist Church where you have been a member for the past forty years.

Current Situation

Eileen comes home from school with an assigned project. She must do a family tree and history and interview as many family members as possible. You are not certain what to tell Eileen.

The teacher tells you that Eileen should have counseling and that she can recommend a very good one. The counselor will only charge $40 per hour. She also comments that Eileen's clothes are old fashioned and don't fit well. You do not tell her that you make most of her clothes. The teacher suggests that you encourage Eileen to invite friends over, but you are not sure anyone would come or if you can stand the noise.

What are Eileen and Wisteria's resources?

Luke

Background

You are a white male, 17-years-old, a junior in high school. You live with your mother and father in a large house with domestic staff. You are the oldest of three children and the only son. Your father grew up in a very wealthy family, attended an Ivy League university, and is currently the president of an international company. He travels a lot, but when he is home he takes you to the club and attends all of your sporting events. Your mother does important work with several charities and political organizations. She is a member of the local City Council and is very involved at the church your family attends.

You make good grades and study hard. You and your sisters have cars, get an allowance, and receive regular reports from your trusts. When you are not practicing basketball, doing volunteer work at church, or studying to keep your 4.5 GPA, you go out with the same friends you have had since grade school. You made some new friends at a party last week; they were fun, and you are planning to get together with them at a party next weekend. You have been thinking about colleges and what you would like to do when you graduate.

Current Situation

For as long as you can remember, your father has talked about how great it will be to have you attending his alma mater, which is also the school his father attended. After you visit the campus, it is clear that a different university will be your choice. You thought about letting your grades go, but think your dad would get you into the college anyway, and if your grades are bad, you will not be accepted at other schools. You made an appointment with your AP teacher because your GPA in his class has dropped to a 4.0.

You really like the kids you met at the party. When you told your parents about your weekend plans, they were concerned. Because they don't know the boys or their families, they will not let you attend the party.

> What are Luke's resources?

* * *

All of the scenarios illustrate patterns and variations of resources found in different economic realities. Several of the scenarios have aspects unique to poverty. All were chosen to help identify and consider options.

Hidden rules in poverty are demonstrated when Oprah is at church and immediately asked to share money. Middle class puts a great deal of emphasis on being self-sufficient and planning. In poverty there are always emergencies and needs. Any spare money is shared. A hidden rule of the support system is that Oprah will share the money; if she doesn't, the next time she needs money her friends will not share with her. In poverty relationships with people are the most important things people have. People must share resources and rely on each other.

Opie and Eileen represent the growing number of children being raised by grandparents. The trend toward nontraditional, highly mobile families is demonstrated when the information Eileen needs to draw a traditional family tree is not available.

Shawnise, Habib, Emerson, and Geraldo present different sets of rules. One set of rules for home, another for the street, at work, and in school. Shawnise and Emerson are acting as adults at home, yet they are expected to act as children at school. Shawnise's physical resources are mentioned. Even though she is hungry most of the time, she must consume the food that *is* available *when* it is available. Planning a menu and purchasing specific types of food would require additional resources.

Kate, Emerson, and Shawnise all provide insights into children who have taken on roles as adults. *A system is a group in which individuals have rules, roles, and relationships.* Emerson and Shawnise are acting in roles as adults and as support systems for their brothers and sisters. Systems include schools, work, home, agencies, and groups. Can you think of other systems? Which systems might be available for use by Kate, Habib, Emerson, and Shawnise? What are the reasons they would use them? What are the reasons they would not?

Kate, Emerson, and Shawnise are examples of the growing number of young people who are living on their own. Children who must take on the roles of adults early may be independent and capable but may have limited resources. Children without access to caring adults or individuals who will teach and explain appropriate roles, relationships, and behaviors must rely on their own resources and skills. These resources and skills can be developed at any age and are discussed in later chapters. Young people in foster care must develop resources that allow them to support themselves by the time they turn 18 and "age out" of the system.

Emotional resources are often developed by seeing how role models handle adverse situations and deal with social interactions. Eileen does not want to be like her mother, and Emerson does not want to be like his father. When there is not an appropriate role model at home, teachers, parents of friends, mentors, social workers, or clergy can serve as role models. Role models can be an individual you know personally or someone you observe in a movie, book, or in your community. Role models can be positive or negative and provide examples of what behaviors and responses look and feel like. To have emotional resources that are healthy, one needs to have an identity. You use role models to help build that identity. Emerson has a relationship with the counselor at school who listens and provides support and encouragement, thus providing a positive role model and emotional support.

The Habib scenario is included to make a point about patterns, roles, and violence in poverty. In wealth the pattern is that negotiation, networks, and connections provide security. In middle class, parents as providers keep the family safe and secure, and identity is related to occupation. When jobs are lost and new job opportunities are limited or nonexistent, identities and resources change. Environments, support systems, and patterns are different. In poverty the pattern is that the providers must work hard, often physically, when jobs are available. As protectors they must have the ability to physically defend themselves and their families. Habib assumed the role of protector when his mother was beaten up.

The Geraldo scenario speaks to similar patterns and environments. Gangs are a type of support system and may be used to defend turf or family. Middle class uses space as a way to deal with differences and disagreements. Generally there is enough space in middle class homes that individuals can to go to a different room to avoid disagreements. Houses are situated in neighborhoods on lots large enough that people can maintain distance. In poverty separation may not be an option. Headphones may be the only way to find a quiet space in a crowed or loud environment. Situations and responses are based on the resources that are available. When resources such as physical space and the language to communicate and negotiate are available, conflicts are handled differently than when those resources are unavailable.

Middle class decisions are driven by achievement and security. Planning and being proactive are valued. Individuals in poverty often live in the tyranny of the moment and must be able to react quickly in order to survive. Habib demonstrates a belief in fate and destiny often seen in poverty. Middle class believes that individuals control their destinies and can change them through changes in behavior. In wealth reactions and decisions are made using networks and connections.

The term "magazine mentality" refers to the premise that if you lack resources to plan or save enough money to buy something big, you will buy little things instead, like magazines, candy, etc., to make yourself feel good. Stores and credit card companies count on this. The ability to plan comes from being able to see a pattern. If you can see a pattern, you can use that pattern to predict what will happen. If you can predict, you can develop a plan. Using a plan and working toward a future picture can help you avoid a magazine mentality. Doing or buying something today that will make you feel good can have consequences that are painful tomorrow. Habib went with his friends to the pawnshop because it sounded good at the time. The consequences were painful.

Luke's scenario represents the hidden rules and patterns seen in generational wealth. Security and connections are an issue when he makes new friends outside of his family network. In middle class education is a way to ensure security and achievement. In wealth education is a way to carry on traditions or a legacy and is used to maintain old networks and develop new ones. Luke's mother does not work at a traditional job, but she is very involved in philanthropic activities and community organizations.

Geraldo wonders what it would be like to live the way Tony does. Tony and Luke both live with hidden rules and expectations. There is an assumption that if an individual has enough money, they have everything they need and want. Remember, one resource that can't be purchased is a relationship of mutual respect. Luke's family has expectations about behavior and achievement, as shown in the need to appeal a 4.0 grade point. Driving forces in middle class relate to patterns of performance or achievement, and resources are used to develop a child's skills and talents.

Using what you know ...   *A Little Quiz*

What resource has the greatest influence on being a lifelong learner?

Which resource can't be purchased?

Which resource has the greatest influence on lifelong stability?

Which resource has the greatest impact on the success of a student at school?

Why is it so important to have spiritual resources?

Why would emotional resources be extremely important at school and work?

What is an internal resource?

What is an external resource?

Which resource is the most important in order to live well?

Resources available to individuals are as unique as the person and the situation.

Use the same pattern found in each of the scenarios you reviewed on the previous pages to write a scenario about your own life. Case scenarios are a skeleton of the story.

BACKGROUND: Set the stage by stating the facts. You are___ years old, _____, and are_____ ...

Keep this in scenario form, include facts, and omit details which will make it harder to identify resources.

CURRENT SITUATION: Write what is happening right now. What are your concerns? What are your resources related to a future picture?

Review the patterns, decide if you should or could change anything, and identify what resources are available. Use the list below to assess which of the eight resources are available. Put a check in the YES column for resources that are present, a check in the NO column if they are not, a check in the column with the question mark if you are uncertain.

RESOURCES	YES	NO	?
Financial			
Emotional			
Mental			
Spiritual			
Physical			
Role Models			
Relationships of Mutual Respect			
Support System			
Hidden Rules			

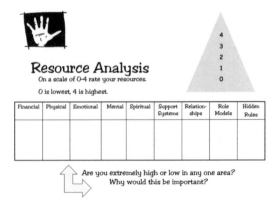

Resource Analysis

On a scale of 0-4 rate your resources.

0 is lowest, 4 is highest.

Financial	Physical	Emotional	Mental	Spiritual	Support Systems	Relation-ships	Role Models	Hidden Rules

Are you extremely high or low in any one area? Why would this be important?

After you have completed the inventory, use a rubric to rate your resources. Ask someone you trust to review the evaluation and point out resources or options you might have missed or overrated. Check to see what resources are available any time you are planning or problem solving. Since situations and circumstances change, check your resources monthly to see patterns and progress using the form in this chapter.

Develop a rubric to clarify what each resource would look like.
Use a scale of 1–4, 1 for the lowest amount and 4 for the highest.

	1	2	3	4
Financial				
Physical				
Emotional				
Mental				
Spiritual				
Support Systems				
Role Models				
Relationships				
Hidden Rules				

Money can be used to purchase other resources.

Financial

Having funds or money to purchase services or goods.

"I didn't have money when I was growing up, I made it."

Eighty-five to 90% of lottery winners are in worse financial shape five years after winning.

Factors: educational attainment of the adults in the home, family structure, addiction issues of the adults in the home, language issues, immigration, and use of money.

What resource(s) cannot be purchased?
Which is more important: The amount of money, or how it is used?
List challenges related to having high monetary resources.

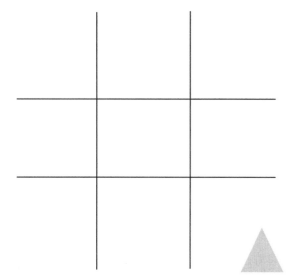

Like cars, physical resources have different styles. What is your style? Are you well-maintained, clean, get regular checkups, and use good fuel? Or do you ignore the oil and buy new paint? Buy additives?

Physical

Having physical health and mobility. In order to be independent or self-sufficient, individuals must be capable of caring for themselves physically and moving around under their own power.

Basically a body that works, is mobile, allows an individual to earn a living, learn, and take care ofhim-/herself without help.

Can you move, walk, and take care of yourself?
Do your physical resources allow you work and learn?
What resources are needed to maintain physical resources?

Emotional

Being able to choose and control emotional responses, particularly to negative situations, without engaging in self-destructive behavior. An internal resource. Ability to learn from role models and relationships. Emotional strength to cope in uncomfortable and new situations.

stamina, perseverance, choices

- ➤ Be alone when times are tough
- ➤ Not engage in destructive behavior
- ➤ Has self-discipline, not impulsive
- ➤ Stay out of a bad situation and not return
- ➤ Habits of persistence and stamina
- ➤ Has a future picture
- ➤ Positively handles peer pressure

What is destructive behavior?

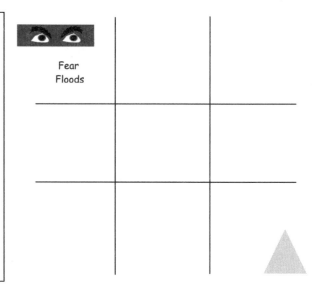

Fear
Floods

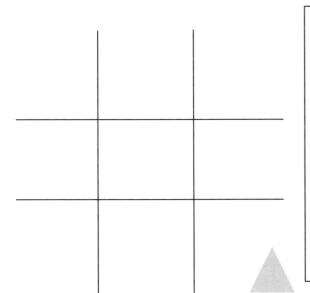

Mental

Reading, Writing, and Computing
Having the mental abilities and acquired skills to deal with daily life and to use information that allows independence, safety, protection from being cheated, and a level of self-sufficiency.

- ➢ Ability to plan
- ➢ Problem solving
- ➢ Identify patterns
- ➢ Literacy

An assumption: Everyone can read, write, add, and subtract.

Hope is that feathered being that lives deep within our soul, calling us to purpose and reminding us of possibilities.

Spiritual

Believing in a divine purpose and guidance. Hope, purpose, a future picture, a power greater than oneself, and/or affiliation with a religious organization.

Do you believe you are valuable and that your actions can make a difference?

Support Systems

Having friends, family, and backup resources available to access in times of need. These are external resources. Individuals who help when you are out of time, need information, help with homework, or someone to talk to without asking you to engage in destructive behavior.

Seven strategies that are used as support systems:

➢Information and know-how. Knowing who to ask and how to get help.

➢Coping strategies—humor, self-talk, mindsets

➢Problem solving opinions—ways to see things differently

➢Relief or assistance when you have done your best and still need help.

➢Positive self-talk: the small voice inside our heads that encourages.

➢Procedural self-talk: the steps to complete a task.

➢Goal-setting and having a future picture.

Who can you count on that won't ask you to engage in destructive behavior? Do you have a support system in place that allows you to devote the time needed to learn, earn, and succeed?

Support systems are networks of relationships.

Relationships and Role Models

Having access to adult(s) who are appropriate, who care, and who do not engage in destructive behavior.

Relationships are personal inter-actions and connections to other human beings. In relationships there is usually an agreed upon set of behaviors, rules, and roles. Relationships are as unique as the individuals, time, and place in which they occur.

Role models are the individuals that we know, read about, or observe and use to model our own actions and behavior.

Do you have a mentor or role models?
Who cares about you and who do you care about?

Role Models, Relationships, and Support Systems

Who ... do you want to be like?
      do you know that has know-how and will teach you?
      can you talk to that can help you see options?
      do you know that will listen and cares?
      will not ask you to engage in destructive behavior?
      will support your development and growth?

How does your work today relate to your future?
Are there negative role models?

When support systems are out of balance,
the individual will be required to give up something.

When one person is always the giver and
the other person is always the taker,
is the relationship one of *mutual respect?*
Why or why not?

Knowledge of Hidden Rules

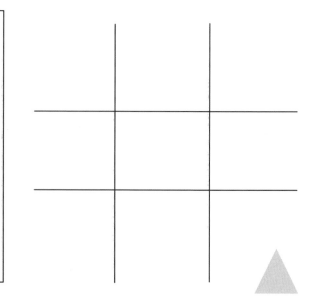

➢ Knowing there are unspoken cues and behaviors
    used and expected by different groups.

➢ Understanding how hidden rules can influence behavior
    and mindsets.

➢ Hidden rules are unwritten and usually unspoken.

➢ Helpful in understanding others. Knowledge of the hidden
    rules should <u>never</u> be used to judge others.

Schools and work use the patterns and
hidden rules of middle class. Why?

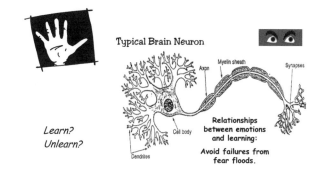

Typical Brain Neuron

Myelin sheath

Axon

Synapses

Cell body

Dendrites

Relationships between emotions and learning:

Avoid failures from fear floods.

Learn?
Unlearn?

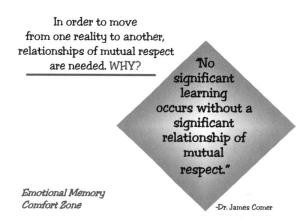

In order to move
from one reality to another,
relationships of mutual respect
are needed. WHY?

Emotional Memory
Comfort Zone

"No significant learning occurs without a significant relationship of mutual respect."

–Dr. James Comer

Comfort Zone

This term describes the emotional safety individuals have when they are in a familiar place and feel safe and secure inside the boundaries or limits of the situation.

"Emotional memory bank" is a term or mental model for the stockpile of emotional memories or experiences stored in the mind. When an event, new information, or behavior occurs, the mind goes directly to its memory banks and automatically connects the current situation to prior information and experiences, then decides how to respond. Connections are made to the intellectual memory and the emotional memory. The emotional memory is the database for the comfort zone. Since all learning is double coded—emotional and intellectual—a conscious effort may be required to sort between emotional and intellectual information—to separate the *current* event from feelings or emotions of a *past* event. The ability to sort and use emotional memory to understand comfort zones is a resource.

Deposits		Withdrawals
Financial		
Emotional ★ Quotations		
		Tickets for Guilt Trips
Mental		
Spiritual		
Physical		
Support System		
Role Models		
Relationships		
Hidden Rules		

Resource Bank Account
Make regular deposits and avoid overdrafts

The Resource Project

As a group, develop a list of resources that are needed in your community. Develop two lists, one list of resources that are available, and another of resources that are needed. By the end of this course, complete your research and develop a list of resources that are available and how to access them. Post the list on the school or community website and publish and distribute the list to local youth. Use the mental models created in the Realities section to review different patterns and resources in your community.

Resources change according to situations and circumstance. Every individual has unique resources, talents, and skills. The greater the resources, the easier it is to respond to a situation or make a change. Identify and increase your resources in order to live well, reach your goals, and share what you learn along the way to help others do the same.

When assessing resources
use these four areas: ————————→
ask what, why, and how
list how improvements can be made in each
refer to the chart on page 48.

Political and Economic
Structures

Exploitation

Human and Social Capital

Individual

Quotations are a resource that can be used to
inspire and develop positive self-talk.
Add your favorites to those listed in the References section.

"How wonderful it is that nobody need wait a single moment
before beginning to improve the world."
–Anne Frank

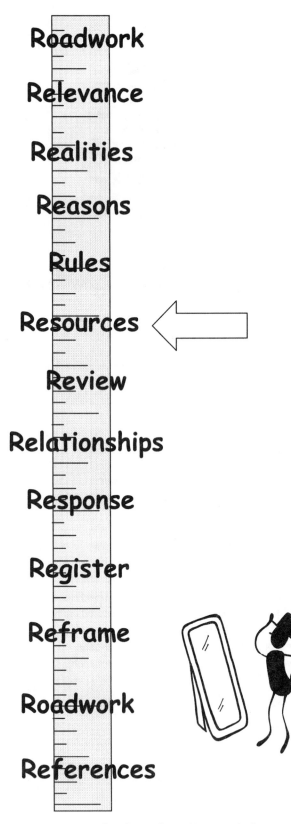

Roadwork

Relevance

Realities

Reasons

Rules

Resources ⬅

Review

Relationships

Response

Register

Reframe

Roadwork

References

What did you learn?
Why is it important?
How will you use this information?

The fox had a million good ideas and the crane only had one. The difference was that the crane put her good idea into action. Do you know anyone like the fox? A person who talks and talks, makes fun of others, and has a million ideas? Make sure you have one good idea that will let you *fly* if you need to.

REFLECTION: If you were to improve or develop one resource that could make the biggest difference in your life, that would help you have, do, or be what you want, what would it be?

It is not just the cards you draw,
but how you play those cards.

CARD OF FATE

You just received a credit card in the mail, issued in your name. The card has a credit limit of $2,000.

What is the current situation?_____

What is the reality of the current situation?_____

_____

Is this important? Why or why not? _____

Do I need to respond? How long can I wait before I respond? How will I respond? _____

_____

What are possible actions, options, or solutions?_____

_____

What resources are available? _____

What resources are missing? _____

Will a different resource work?_____

How can I get this resource?_____

What response will I try?_____

Why will this work?_____

Why won't it work?_____

How will I know it worked?_____

What else will I try if it doesn't work? Plan B:_____

_____

_____

Chapter 7 REVIEW

What is this: Review literally means to view again; to look at, study, or examine with the intent of making an addition or change. Realities were defined earlier as the way things actually are or the way we believe them to be. Another word for the way we believe things to be or view them is *paradigm*. In this chapter we will look at realities and mindsets to see new points of view, paradigms, and mental models.

Thomas Kuhn, an American scientist, studied and wrote his observations of members of communities sharing beliefs and ways of doing things. The label he used to talk about them was *paradigm*, a Greek term used in science. Paradigms, like realities, are the point of view or how individuals see the world. Like realities, paradigms can be how things really are as well as how we believe them to be. The mind sorts information based on patterns, mental models, and paradigms. Stephen Covey defines a paradigm as a mental map a person uses to understand and navigate the world. Ruby Payne defines a mental model as the way the mind holds information and concepts in an abstract form; a mental blueprint, picture, or story of how things are that can be used as a reference to sort information against.

Paradigm shift describes what takes place when individuals discover new information that is so profound or different from their mental model or paradigm that it changes the way they understand or believe their world to be. The new information causes them to see the world in a different way, and the picture in the mind is changed. These are "aha! moments." They allow us to break from old patterns, to change our view regarding in-the-box or limited thinking, our scripts, and our assumptions by seeing other viewpoints, options, and possibilities.

Why this is important: Paradigms are used to sort information. Like hidden rules they are generally unwritten and unspoken and accepted as the way things are. If you have been told you are a chicken your whole life, you may not realize you are really an eagle. Fish have difficulty seeing water. It is important to review and think about how you see yourself, your limits, roles, and options. What you believe, your reality or paradigm about yourself and others, may cause you to accept limits and overlook options and resources that could help you reach your goal, dream, or future picture.

How can you use this information: Learn to see and think about people, things, and situations from more than one frame of reference or viewpoint; leave the dance floor and go to the balcony; look first in the mirror and then out the window. Look in the mirror and ask yourself what part of a situation is internal, owned, or controlled by you. Look out the window to ask what part is external, controlled by others. Look for humor and options in situations. Watch how other people use their talents, stamina, and courage to live well and make contributions. Use role models, scenarios, and stories to build resources and help establish your own personal identity. Build resources, use what you know and learn, have courage to see new options, develop a future picture, step out of your comfort zone, and pursue your dreams.

The ability to review or "think different" requires mental and emotional resources. Asking a question, finding humor, and seeing options require the ability to sort information and are skills that can be developed. Good comedians and storytellers are able to flip information and talk about things that may be very serious in a way that reveals humor and different paradigms.

A comedian was checking into the hospital where he was scheduled to have heart surgery. A reporter asked him how long he would have to stay. He replied, "About two weeks if things go well, a couple of hours if they don't go so well."

> **"We cannot solve the significant problems we face today at the same level of thinking we were at when we created them."** —Albert Einstein

While waiting in the office of an elementary school to pick up children, an elderly man told me, "Children are not important today." Shocked by the statement because my children are the most important thing in my life, I asked him to explain what he meant. "When I was growing up, I was very important. I came home every day and chopped and stacked wood. If I didn't, my family did not have wood to stay warm, and my mother could not cook. I was very important, but kids today don't do things like that. They are not allowed to be important."

How do you see yourself?

THE EAGLE CHICK

The eagle saw his world through the eyes of a chicken. Even though he had unique resources that would have allowed him to soar far above the earth, he was unable to see new options, patterns, or possibilities. He accepted the limits of the reality he knew. If he had been able to make the connection and had tried to fly, the chickens might have laughed at him, so he played it safe and stayed in his comfort zone.

 Reverend Otis Moses said: "I have often wondered what would have happened when Patrick Henry stood up and proclaimed, 'Give me liberty or death!' if all of his slaves would have stood up and shouted, *'Yes! Give us our liberty too!'"*

In the book *A Tree Grows in Brooklyn,* the main character is a girl named Francie. When her family moves into their Brooklyn apartment, their dream is to save enough money to purchase and own a piece of land in America. A small tin can bank is nailed to the floor in the corner of the closet, and the family saves every extra penny to make their dream come true. When Francie's father dies suddenly, she and her mother are faced with a new reality and have to find money to pay for his funeral. The situation is compounded when the undertaker, who has already been paid for her father's funeral service, tells Francie she still owes him for the cemetery plot. When she asks the cost, the man tells her it will cost 20 dollars.

The story continues: "Francie pried up the tin bank from the back of the closet and placed it on the table. There was $18.62, which the undertaker took as full payment. After 14 years the old tin can was battered and the paint worn away. 'Mama, do you want me to nail it back down in the closet?' asked Francie. 'No,' said Mama, slowly folding the deed to the cemetery plot. 'We don't need it anymore. You see Francie, we finally own a bit of land in America.'"

"We see the world not as it is, but as we are."
–Stephen Covey

How are paradigms, realities, patterns, and hidden rules the same? How do economic realities and resources influence paradigms?

Consider the paradigm shifts that must or will occur if …
      you are the first person in your family going to college.
      you have never seen a plant grow from a seed that has been buried in the ground.
      you understand there are many resources in addition to money.
      you accept that people have different ways of doing and thinking about things.

      What do you need to learn? What do you need to unlearn?

Watch the slide show: All of these people are recognized for their accomplishments or contributions.
Some of them faced language barriers. Some had learning disabilities.
Some came from poverty, some came from wealth.
Some were immigrants.
Each of them overcame challenges.
Each of them discovered a talent and developed it.
Any of them could serve as a role model or hero.
All of them had the courage to think different,
the ability to see themselves as they might be,
the resources to dream of what could be,
and the courage to say I will be …

Do you?

Write or draw a personal aha! moment. *Aha! moments* are the experiences of a person who suddenly sees the whole picture in a different way.

Sir Isaac Newton:
"If I have seen further, it is by standing
on the shoulders of giants that came before me."

A Free Fall

1. One *thing* that makes you **furious.**
2. Something you think is **funny.**
3. One *thing* you **fear.**
4. Who could you **forgive?**
5. One thing you do that is **fabulous!**
6. Three qualities of a **friend.**
7. What do you have **faith** in?
8. If you could **fix** anything, what would it be?
9. What do you think of when you think of **freedom?**
10. What would you try if you knew you could not **fail?**
11. Paint a picture of your **future:** daily, weekly, monthly.
12. What would you do if it was **free?**

Missions and purpose sometimes develop out of strong feelings and beliefs held by an individual. Things that are important enough to make us furious can generate energy that can be used in a positive way. Use the information here to consider work, careers, and jobs that would be interesting to you. Use your unique talents and experiences to make a difference. Knowing what you would fix can also help sort options, see patterns, find a purpose, or determine a career. Knowing what you fear and why can help you build a future picture and develop resources to deal with challenges.

You are 30 years old ...
What do you want to be,
do,
and have?

"Too often we are scared.
Scared of what we might not be able to do.
Scared of what people might think if we tried.
We let our fears stand in the way of our hopes.
We say no when we ought to say yes.
We sit quietly when we want to scream.
And we shout with the others when we ought to keep our mouths shut. Why?"
-Barry Sanders

To address this situation, should you look in the mirror or out the window?

Mental models: How do you see yourself? What is your paradigm or reality? We use pictures and mental models to store abstract information and patterns in our minds. These become mental models, our paradigms, or how view or see ourselves.

Self-talk: People have a little voice inside their heads that talks to them. This little voice can give encouraging messages and positive affirmations or negative messages, but both help develop and support the mental picture we have of ourselves and our future picture. Self-talk provides steps and support to finish tasks and get through difficult situations.

Ways to develop this resource are writing a mission or belief statement; positive affirmations; listing steps needed to complete a task, reach a goal, and encourage along the way; or reading quotes that inspire and guide. Use any of these by reading or stating them daily, and before a test or any important event.

A little quiz:

Rate yourself.
You are the only person who will see the answers.
A: Always, I am doing great!
B: Usually, I do pretty well.
C: Sometimes, I get by.
D: Not usually, I could do better.
F: Never, I need to improve.

_____ I always have control over my life.
_____ My support systems are not out of balance.
_____ My behavior is true to me, not swayed by peers.
_____ I can usually figure out where I need to go.
_____ I believe I have skills and talents worth developing.
_____ I accept that it is my responsibility to change my life.
_____ I am making plans for what I want to become in life.
_____ I challenge myself to try new things and take positive risks.
_____ I have a healthy self-confidence.
._____ I keep my promises.
_____ I am good at managing relationships.
_____ I feel good about myself and my actions.
_____ I make decisions that are well thought out.
_____ I can control my impulses.
_____ My grades are good enough; they don't stress me or my family out.
_____ I am a hard worker.
_____ I do a good job of using my resources.
_____ I have a positive adult role model.
_____ I replay my victories mentally and use positive self-talk.
_____ I use organizational skills to get things done.
_____ I use coping strategies before I go out the side door.
_____ I have habits that benefit my physical resources.

I can_____
I will_____
I am_____
I believe_____
I am good at_____
I have choices about_____
I was successful at_____
I have faith in_____
I have unique talents and skills.
I am in control of my emotions.
I am learning more each day.
I am grateful for_____
_____cares about me and I care about her/him.
I am respectful of others and live in peace.
I was astounded when I was able to_____

Eliminate negative self-talk!

Write the names of three people who have influenced you in a positive way.

1._____

2._____

3._____

Write the name of one person you admire.

_____

List two attributes or qualities this person has that you admire most.

_____

_____

How are you like this person?

1. First I will:
2. Then I will:
3. Next I will:

If we did all the things we are capable of doing, we would literally astound ourselves.
-Thomas Edison

"We must not cease from exploration, and the end of our exploration will be to arrive where we began and know the place for the first time."   -T. S. Eliot
Keep listening, looking, laughing, and learning.

What did you learn?
Why is it important?
How will you use it?

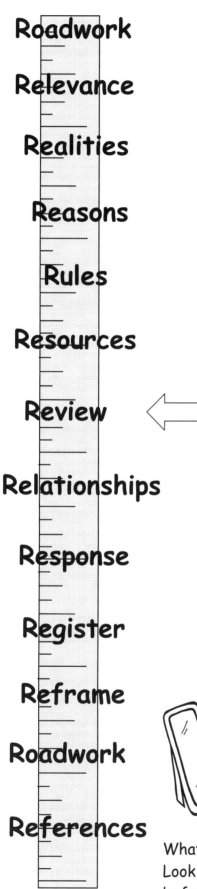

Roadwork

Relevance

Realities

Reasons

Rules

Resources

Review ←

Relationships

Response

Register

Reframe

Roadwork

References

Define:
A mentor
A role model
A hero

Here's to the crazy ones.
The misfits ... the rebels ...
The round pegs in square holes.
The ones who see things differently.

They are not fond of rules,
because they change things.

They invent, they imagine, they heal.
They explore, they create, they inspire.

While some call them crazy, others see genius.
Because people who are crazy enough
to think they can change the world
are the ones who do.

What will you do?

-adapted from Apple Computers

What do you see?
Look in the mirror at least one time
before walking through any door.

It is not just the cards you draw,
but how you play those cards.

CARD OF FATE

You have just received your dream invitation. It is to the place or event you always wanted to go to. All expenses are paid. Will you go? How will you prepare?

What is the current situation?_____

What is the reality of the current situation?_____

_____

Why is this important, and is it a problem?_____

Do I need to respond? How long can I wait before I respond? How will I respond?_____

_____

What are possible actions, solutions or options?_____

_____

What resources are available?_____

What resources are missing?_____

Will a different resource work?_____

How can I get this resource?_____

What response will I try?_____

Why will this work?_____

Why won't it work?_____

How will I know it worked?_____

What else will I try if it doesn't work? Plan B:_____

_____

Notes

Chapter 8
RELATIONSHIPS

Rules + Regulations - Relationships = Resentment + Refusal
Rules + Rigor + Relationships = Resources + Results + Respect

What they are: Relationships are the connections, patterns, and interactions between people or things. They are personal and interpersonal and exist throughout the universe. Every relationship is as unique as the individual, situation, time, or place in which it occurs. *Relationships are to resources what an engine is to a car: the driving force.* The mind uses relationships and patterns to sort, process, and store information.

Why this is important: Relationships greatly influence the reasons we do things and our purpose in life. It is through relationships that we learn from and about others and develop networks that encourage, inspire, support, and teach us. Relationships influence both the development of resources as well as how we use them. Understanding patterns and relationships can be the difference between success and failure in the classroom, at work, and in life. Learning relationships are both emotional and mental, are "double coded," and what we learn is always influenced by the relationship with who we are learning it from and what we are learning it for. Using relationships to develop mental models and see patterns can make learning easier and faster and allows individuals to predict and then plan.

How can you use this information: Learn about and understand hidden rules and resources in various environments and systems. Observe role models and patterns of behavior that can be used to understand others and choose responses, coping strategies, and behaviors of your own. Develop and maintain relationships of mutual respect in order to learn and live well. Make regular deposits into the relationship bank accounts of others as well as your own. Understand and use the relationships between current tasks and situations to help make decisions and build resources as you work toward a future picture and story.

David in chapter 2 needed a relationship of mutual respect to help him understand a system and connect the resources available. Moving between groups or economic classes is considerably easier when a relationship of trust and respect is in place to inspire, help through the changes, and provide information needed to avoid emotional tension or embarrassment. We all have a *comfort zone,* the emotional or physical safety people have when they are in a familiar place or situation and feel safe and secure inside the limits or boundaries. Comfort zones can be physical places but most often refer to emotions and the comfort or discomfort that occurs when individuals are outside the accepted norms, patterns, or hidden rules they know.

Its fun to go where everybody knows your name ...

Why are relationships so important?

Comfort Zone
Emotional Memory
Role Models
Support Systems
Prior Learning and Knowledge

| Survival Relationships Entertainment | Work Achievement Material Security | Political, Financial, and Social Connections |

"No significant learning occurs without a significant relationship."
–Dr. James Comer

(relationships of mutual respect)

JUVENILE or CHILD = a person 18 years of age or younger

Children who must take on roles as adults early must be independent, but may have limited resources.

Appropriate role models to observe and learn from may not be available. If this is the case, the *child* who is acting as the *adult* is left to **guess** at what appropriate behavior and relationships are.

To improve this situation, the child must work to develop emotional resources, relationships of mutual respect, and role models. Stamina will be required to decode and determine which behaviors and resources are appropriate and when to use them.

Role Models
Support Systems
Mediation ⟶

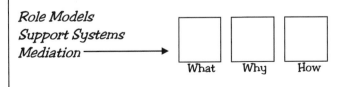

What   Why   How

Five Reasons individuals leave poverty or their comfort zone:

It is too painful to stay, or they are removed.
They have compelling goals and know what they want to do, be, or have.
They have a special talent or skill that takes them to new surroundings or situations.
They have a key relationship of mutual respect that inspires and supports the move.
They are able to get an education.

Examples ...

_____
_____
_____
_____
_____
_____

Rules + Rigor + Relationships = Resources and Resiliency

Resiliency is the capacity to spring back, rebound, successfully adapt in the face of adversity, and develop social competence despite exposure to extreme stress.

adapted from *The Resilient Self* by Steven J. Wolin Sybil Wolin

Seven resources for resiliency in relationships:

Insight: Ask the tough questions. Why?
Independence: Keep distance emotionally and physically.
Relationships: mutual respect
Initiative: Take charge of problems, stretch your abilities.
Creativity: Find beauty, order, a purpose, and a vision.
Humor: Find comedy in the tragic; ability to reframe.
Morality: Staying holy in unholy places.

Ask yourself:
What is this situation?
Why does it exist, why did it occur?
How is this situation not about me?
With whom do I have mutual respect?
What part can I address? What can I control?
What are the rules here? What is my purpose?
What about this is funny?
What is the right thing to do?
What is the least destructive, kindest way?

Future picture, roles, and steps: what, why, how

1) Identify a future picture. 2) Define your role. 3) Set a step to improve each role.

Picture: <u>NBA</u> Role: <u>Guard</u> Step: <u>50 free throws every day</u>

Picture:__Role: __Step:_____

Picture:__Role: __Step:_____

Picture:__Role: __Step:_____

Picture:__Role: __Step:_____

Picture:__Role: __Step:_____

Always check the relationship of roles, goals, and steps to your future picture.
Future pictures, goals, and roles change.

I'll be there for you ...

Most important qualities in a friend:

When one person is always the giver, and the other person is always the taker, resentment will occur. Why?

For additional insights read: *Crossing the Tracks for Love* by Ruby Payne

A future picture

Write deposits to your personal relationship account in each circle.

Build intellectual capital

What do you want to do, be, or have?
Start being what you want to be right now!

What isn't working?
Tough question ... honest answer.

Why isn't it working?

Are expectations realistic?
Are expectations the same?
Assumptions?
Mental Models?
Hidden Rules?

How will we change this?

My part ...

Your part ...

Date we will check back:

Relationship Rx

What past experiences did you bring on this trip as baggage from previous relationships?

R + R + R = R + R + R

DEPOSITS	WITHDRAWALS
Seek first to understand	Seek first to be understood
Keeping promises	Breaking promises
Kindnesses, courtesies	Unkindnesses, discourtesies
Clarifying expectations	Violating expectations
Loyalty to the absent	Disloyalty, duplicity
Apologies	Pride, conceit, arrogance
Open to feedback	Rejecting feedback

from *The Seven Habits of Highly Effective People* by Stephen Covey

R Rules Relationship Bank Account

DEPOSITS	WITHDRAWALS
Acceptance of what the individual cannot say about a person or situation	Insistence and demands for full explanation about person or situation
Respect for the demands and priorities of relationships	Put-downs or sarcasm about the humor or individual
Appreciation of humor and entertainment provided by the individual	Insistence on the middle class view of relationships
Using the adult voice	Using the parent voice
Assisting with goal-setting	Telling the individual his or her goals
Identifying options and planning related to available resources	Making judgments based on the value and availability of resources
Understanding the importance of individual personality, personal freedom, and speech	Assigning character traits that diminish the individual

Using your understanding of the hidden rules, discuss why these are so important. Can you think of others?

The relationship hitmen and -women:

Assumptions
Expectations
Past experiences
Hidden rules
Limited language
Faulty support systems
Negative role models
Backdoor exits
Fixers
Takers

Deposit	Withdrawal
_____	_____
_____	_____
_____	_____
_____	_____
_____	_____
_____	_____
_____	_____

Orville and Wilbur Wright
Ludwig and Alfred Nobel
Helen Keller and Anne Sullivan
Steve Jobs and Steve Wozniak
Christopher Columbus and Queen Isabella

Consider your personal relationships and the differences they make in your life.

Comedians are people who see
relationships and patterns,
hidden rules and reasons,
then reframe them to show connections
and relationships to our lives
that make us laugh.

1. A sound you hear in the morning is:
    a rooster, dogs, elephants, a train
2. What does "cracking a joke" mean?
3. What is a roach?
4. What is a concierge?
5. What is duct tape used for?
6. What is a multiplication table?

Relationships at School
Make deposits of integrity; avoid withdrawals and sarcasm.
Clarify boundaries, expectations, and rules, and agree to live by them.
Use school rules, honor resources of individuals, build support systems,
    respect achievement, use formal register.
Seek role models and relationships of mutual respect that teach and inspire.

$$R + R + R = R + R + R$$

In relationships of mutual respect ...

the role of a student is:

the role of an educator is:

their role together is:

Write a thank you note.

Student challenge:
Marcus Allen says: "Sometimes to make a difference you have to be the difference."

Nine Learning Relationships the what and why

Nine Learning Relationships	how
Language arts: Using structure and language to communicate	
Math: Assigning order and value to the universe	
Biology: Identify living systems and relationships within and among those systems	
Chemistry: Bonding	
Algebra: Solving for the unknown through functions	
Geometry: Using logic to order and assign values to form and space	
Physics: Using matter and energy through math applications	
Social studies: Identifying patterns of people and governments over time	
Earth science: Identifying and predicting physical phenomena	

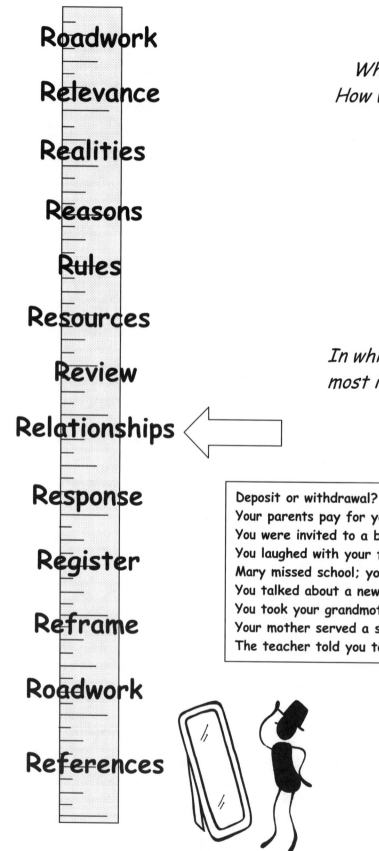

Roadwork

Relevance

Realities

Reasons

Rules

Resources

Review

Relationships

Response

Register

Reframe

Roadwork

References

What did you learn?
Why is it important?
How will you use this information?

In which economic class are relationships
most important? Explain your answer.

Deposit or withdrawal?
Your parents pay for your prom dress but have not seen it.
You were invited to a birthday party but did not go.
You laughed with your friends at the new girl in school.
Mary missed school; you got her homework and took it to her house.
You talked about a new friend with one of your old friends.
You took your grandmother to lunch at a fast food drive-in.
Your mother served a special family recipe for dinner.
The teacher told you to help a girl in class today.

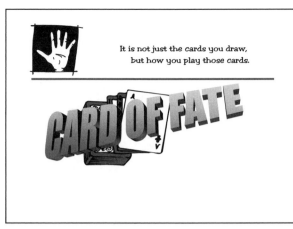

It is not just the cards you draw,
but how you play those cards.

CARD OF FATE

Your boy-/girlfriend's family is *very* different from yours. You really care for him/her.

What is the current situation?_____

What is the reality of the current situation?_____

_____

Is this important? Why or why not?_____

Do I need to respond? How long can I wait before I respond? How will I respond?_____

_____

What are possible actions, options, solutions?_____

_____

What resources are available?_____

What resources are missing?_____

Will a different resource work?_____

How can I get this resource?_____

What response will I try?_____

Why will this work?_____

Why won't it work?_____

How will I know it worked?_____

What else will I try if it doesn't work? Plan B:_____

_____

"Champions do not become champions in the ring, they are just recognized there."
-unknown

What they are: Resources for responding to situations and people. Responses are the way individuals react or acknowledge a person, situation, or event. Responses are as varied as the individual and each situation, but they are always based on the resources available at the time of the response.

Why this is important: Responses are relative to hidden rules, future pictures, resources, and driving forces. Processes and mental models to build resources that allow choice, various options, and help control impulsivity are needed. Individuals with high emotional resources are able to respond with stamina, courage, and resiliency, but when emotional resources are low responses may be impulsive, out of anger or fear, and directed only at the moment.

How you can use this information: Develop resources that support positive responses by using role models and scenarios and understanding patterns of cause and effect and driving forces in economic classes. Use strategies and tools for responding and controlling impulsivity. Situations and systems are complex; resources are interrelated; studying a person or individual behaviors is not the same as studying the systems or issues. Review internal and external resources and research in the table on page 48 in the Reasons chapter. Life is like a card game; you get good hands and you get bad hands. Understanding the rules, knowing which cards to keep or discard, when to draw, and when to fold will determine if you win or lose.

Two men, each diagnosed with a serious illness, shared a room in a hospital. The men talked and shared experiences as they passed the hours. The man assigned to the bed next to the window related all of the activities and scenes that only he could see taking place on the grounds below. Events like a young couple leaving the hospital carrying a new baby, an elderly woman pushing her husband's wheelchair to the garden, and the geese, each identified by a name that matched its personality, that landed on the grass every evening. Days, then weeks passed. When the man in the bed next to the window died, his roommate asked to be moved to the bed near the window so he could once again be a part of the outside world.

His request was granted, and when the move was complete he sat up to look out the window. To his dismay and then amazement, he realized that the window faced a dark red brick wall. For all of the time they had been ill, and through each of those wonderful stories, his friend had simply used his imagination and resources to pass the hours and keep them connected to the world outside their room by making the best of their circumstances.

Victor Frankl wrote in his book *Man's Search for Meaning* about men in the German concentration camps walking through the huts, caring for others, even giving away their last pieces of bread. He goes on to say that even though they were few in number, these men proved to him that every freedom can be taken from a man but one. He states that that one thing, which he calls "the last of human freedoms," was the right in any situation "to choose one's own way." Resources = Choices.

When President John Kennedy was asked by a news reporter how he became a war hero, he replied, "It was involuntary. They sank my boat."

Circle of Control
Resiliency ✓

Arun Ghandi, in an article titled "Reflections of Peace," talks of her father, Mahatma Gandhi, and how when he first arrived in South Africa he was thrown off the train because of the color of his skin. He was so humiliated that he spent the rest of the night wondering what to do in order to get justice for the injustice shown him.

She reports that his first response was anger—an eye for an eye. But he changed his thinking after realizing that that was a response controlled only by his emotions. His second response was to go back to India. In India he was respected, knew the rules, and was accepted. Then he considered a third response, nonviolent action. This remained Gandhi's way his entire life, and he spent 22 years in South Africa working to make a positive difference before he returned to India. Ghandi used his resources to see options and possibilities different than those he first considered. Like Ghandi, in order to succeed, people must use the resources available, control impulses, and consider all the options before responding.

In all of these examples individuals used the resources they had to respond to and meet the unique challenges they faced. Resiliency is developed when individuals are able to see a situation and understand their reality, role, and the rules. It takes emotional resources to work through a situation and then do the thing that is the kindest and least destructive. In the story *Willie the Shoeshine Man*, Willie controlled the only thing he could—himself. Every day the chief set up a different situation designed to make Willie fail. Willie was too smart to let anything—the chief, new circumstances, or his emotions—control him.

Like W. Mitchell says, "It is not what happens to you, it's how you respond to what has happened."

These drawings provide a mental model of responses. The *stimulus* is the event, the **action**, what happened. The *response* is the **reaction**, or how the individual responds to the stimulus, event, or action.

The space between stimulus and response in these mental models represents the time between the action and the reaction.
Use a Force Field tool to help sort responses and consider choices and consequences.

To survive on the street, one must rely upon nonverbal, sensory, and reactive skills.
To survive in school and at work, one must use verbal, abstract, and proactive skills.

| Stimulus What | Response How |

Model 1
Immediate Response
Survival
Emotion
Fight or Flight
Impulsivity

| Stimulus What | Why | Response How |

FREEDOM
FUTURE PICTURE
HIDDEN RULES
RESOURCES

The story I tell myself

Model 2
Time to Respond
Maintain Control
Voice/Register
Sort:
Consequences
Thoughts
Resources
Options
Future Picture

Resources for Responses
- Anger is based on fear. Know what you are afraid of and if the fear is justified.
- Use behaviors that are not destructive to you or to others.
- Choose language and voice.
    Language and words allow conversation and negotiation.
    Language allows individuals to talk about the problem, not the people.
    The child or parent voice will stall the conversation.
- Stay holy in unholy places by doing what is right, most kind, and least destructive.
- Find the humor in the situation.
- Ask what happened, why did it happen, how long can I wait to respond?
- Determine what the hidden rules are, then how you will respond.
- Know the limits, structures, and consequences.

?
School
Street

Choices are governed by the resources available and how they are used,
the ability to see cause and effect, and the consequences an individual is
willing to accept. What are parameters and boundaries?
  Why are they important?
How do these driving forces and hidden rules influence responses? Use the chart on page 48 as a reference.

	POVERTY	MIDDLE CLASS	WEALTH
DRIVING FORCE	*Survival, Relationships, Entertainment*	*Work, Achievement, Material Security*	*Financial, Political, and Social Connections*

On the way home from work, the engine in your car quit.

You won three tickets to a rock concert that will be in your city next month.

Your science teacher is very demanding. He mentioned your attitude in class today.

You had a party at your house, kids were outside talking, dancing, and the music was loud. Neighbor's reaction?

Your boyfriend/girlfriend got paid Friday and wants to borrow money from you. It is Monday.

Why are patterns and structures so important?
  If a person lives in an unpredictable environment,
  using random patterns for choice,
  and has not developed the ability to plan:

If an individual cannot plan, he/she
CANNOT PREDICT

If an individual cannot predict, he/she
CANNOT IDENTIFY CAUSE AND EFFECT

If an individual cannot identify cause and effect, he/she
CANNOT IDENTIFY CONSEQUENCE

If an individual cannot identify consequence, he/she
CANNOT CONTROL IMPULSIVITY

If an individual cannot control impulsivity, he/she
HAS AN INCLINATION TOWARD CRIMINAL BEHAVIOR

Adapted from the work of Reuven Feuerstein

Case studies:
Habib
Teen Pranks
Stop Sign Case

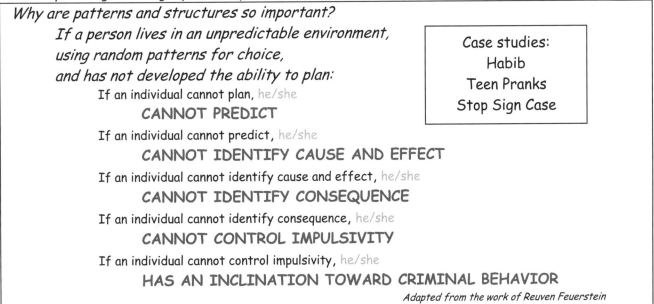

Mediation		
Stimulus	Meaning	Strategy

What was the real meaning?

R + R + R + R + R

Aha!

Follow Quick Responses
By Taking Time for Personal Reflection

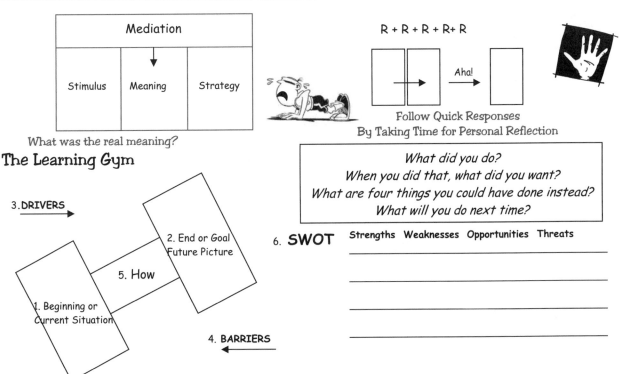

The Learning Gym

3. DRIVERS

2. End or Goal
Future Picture

5. How

1. Beginning or
Current Situation

4. BARRIERS

What did you do?
When you did that, what did you want?
What are four things you could have done instead?
What will you do next time?

6. SWOT Strengths Weaknesses Opportunities Threats
_____
_____
_____
_____

3 Voices x 3

Consider responses to each of these voices ...
    if you are talking to yourself.
    if you are talking to others.
    if someone is talking to you.

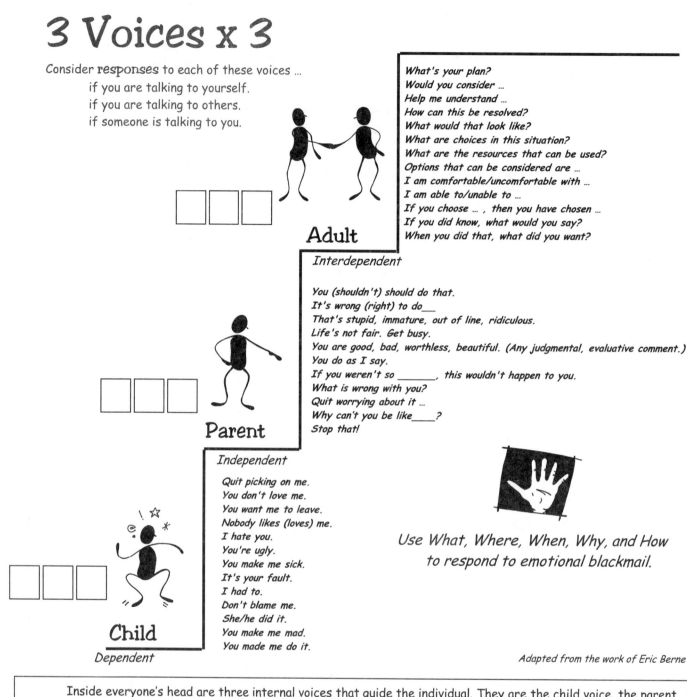

Adult
Interdependent

What's your plan?
Would you consider ...
Help me understand ...
How can this be resolved?
What would that look like?
What are choices in this situation?
What are the resources that can be used?
Options that can be considered are ...
I am comfortable/uncomfortable with ...
I am able to/unable to ...
If you choose ... , then you have chosen ...
If you did know, what would you say?
When you did that, what did you want?

Parent
Independent

You (shouldn't) should do that.
It's wrong (right) to do___
That's stupid, immature, out of line, ridiculous.
Life's not fair. Get busy.
You are good, bad, worthless, beautiful. (Any judgmental, evaluative comment.)
You do as I say.
If you weren't so _____, this wouldn't happen to you.
What is wrong with you?
Quit worrying about it ...
Why can't you be like____?
Stop that!

Child
Dependent

Quit picking on me.
You don't love me.
You want me to leave.
Nobody likes (loves) me.
I hate you.
You're ugly.
You make me sick.
It's your fault.
I had to.
Don't blame me.
She/he did it.
You make me mad.
You made me do it.

*Use What, Where, When, Why, and How
to respond to emotional blackmail.*

Adapted from the work of Eric Berne

Inside everyone's head are three internal voices that guide the individual. They are the child voice, the parent voice, and the adult voice. These little voices are the voices that give you messages, talk you through steps to finish tasks, give encouragement or correction, determine behaviors, and help you negotiate choices.

The voice of the child can be whiny and negative. In general, individuals who talk this way don't take responsibility for their actions, blame others, and are victims. They are easily controlled by others because they don't take control themselves. They will use the child voice to manipulate or to respond in a conflict. This voice stalls communication, but it can also be playful and teasing or may sound immature.

The parent voice is authoritative, direct, and judgmental and comes from a position of power. It is demanding and sometimes threatening. The parent voice can be positive when it is used to stop behavior that is dangerous and is then followed by an adult voice to redirect. Parents use it to teach their children when they take control of the situation, as in, "Get out of the street!" followed by a conversation and directions about how a child should cross the street. The internal parent voice, when it is used in self-talk, can cause shame and guilt, as in, "Why was I so stupid? Can't I even cross the street right? I should have looked both ways; I know I could get hit by a car."

The adult voice allows negotiation. This voice provides a way for information to be examined in a non-threatening way, is used to choose behaviors, get through situations, and talk through tasks. The adult voice talks to the issues and situations, not the individual. Learning the adult voice is a strategy or habit that improves communication and negotiation on all levels.

Which voice makes deposits into your emotional bank account?

Children who function as adults often develop only the child and parent voices and lack the adult voice. The parent voice is often used to discipline or stop behavior, and the conversation then continues in adult voices. If students respond in the child voice, they may sound helpless or unable to take responsibility for their own actions. If students respond using the parent voice, they may sound sarcastic and get in more trouble.

An adult voice is a resource that can be used to deal with emotional memory and hidden rules. Practice procedural and positive self-talk. Learn to respond in a nonjudgmental way, stating facts, outlining steps of a task, or telling yourself you are doing a good job. Learn to address the issue or situation, not the person. When the adult voice is missing, information will not be sorted in a nonjudgmental way. If there is not an adult voice to respond, emotions escalate and hidden rules, fear, and anger take over.

A check sheet is a way to record the frequency of an item or items.

Use the check sheet below to track how many times you use each voice in one week.
Make one tally mark each time you use the child, parent, or adult voice. Use one line for school, the one below it for home.
When you have four tally marks, draw a vertical line through them and count by fives. ǀǀǀǀ
Keep a weekly record. It takes 21 days to develop a habit. Use the Barbell tool to plan work in the Learning Gym.

	CHILD	PARENT	ADULT
Monday			
Tuesday			
Wednesday			
Thursday			
Friday			
Saturday			
Sunday			
Total			

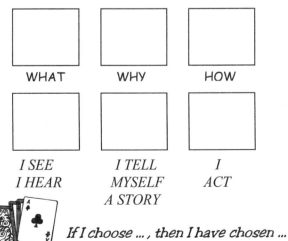

WHAT	WHY	HOW
I SEE *I HEAR*	*I TELL* *MYSELF* *A STORY*	*I* *ACT*

If I choose … , then I have chosen …
If I choose … , then I have chosen …

Which voice does the person you are dating use?

Self-Talk:

Good, bad, or ugly?

How can voice be a resource to build capital?

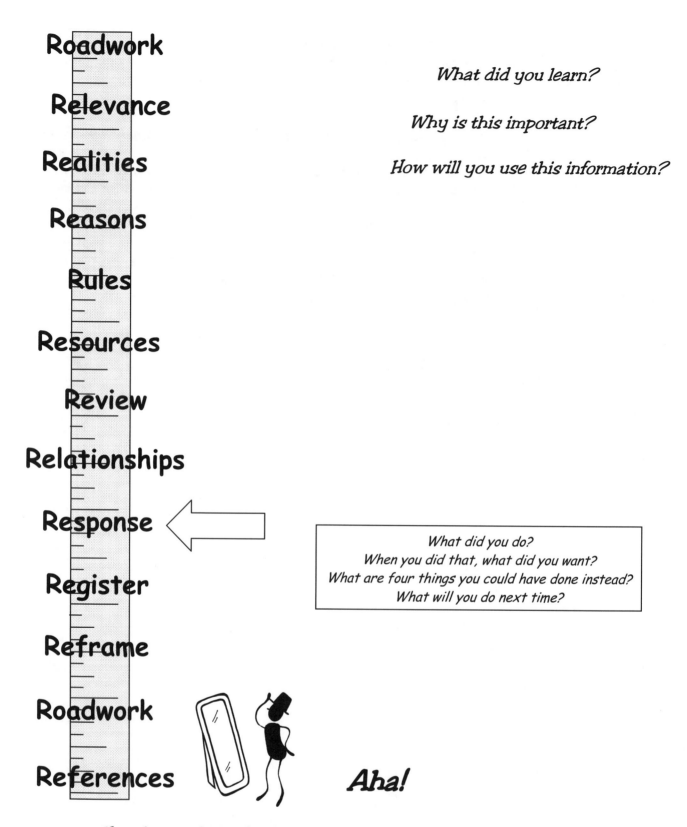

Roadwork

Relevance

Realities

Reasons

Rules

Resources

Review

Relationships

Response ⬅

Register

Reframe

Roadwork

References

What did you learn?

Why is this important?

How will you use this information?

What did you do?
When you did that, what did you want?
What are four things you could have done instead?
What will you do next time?

Aha!

Use what you know about voices to see patterns and how they influence behaviors.
Try different voices with your friends and watch their
responses, both verbal and nonverbal. Be Careful!

It is not just the cards you draw,
but how you play those cards.

CARD OF FATE

Your mother has been arrested,
-or-
Prom is in two weeks and you were
just invited.

What is the reality of the current situation?_____

_____

Is this important? Why or why not? _____

Do I need to respond? How long can I wait before I respond? How will I respond?_____

_____

 What are possible actions, options, solutions?_____

_____

What resources are available? _____

What resources are missing?_____

Will a different resource work?_____

How can I get this resource?_____

What response will I try?_____

Why will this work?_____

Why won't it work?_____

How will I know it worked?_____

What else will I try if it doesn't work? Plan B:_____

_____

"We do not describe the world we see …
we see the world we know how to describe."
–Tim Lucas

Chapter 10
REGISTER

What is this: *Register* refers to the aspects and patterns of language. In 1967 a Dutch linguist named Martin Joos found that every language in the world has five registers: frozen, formal, consultative, casual, and intimate. Each of the five registers uses distinct patterns of word choice, order, and structure. Different registers and patterns of language are seen in each of the three economic classes. Because the hidden rules of middle class are used at school and work, success, achievement, and the ability to communicate and negotiate are largely related to how well an individual can use formal register. There is a direct relationship between one's ability to use language and one's earning power.

Why this is important: Language is the tool we use to share our ideas, our hopes, and our dreams; it provides a system of abstract representations (words, numbers, and symbols) to communicate sensory information. Intelligence on IQ tests, job, and college applications is determined by how well individuals are able to show what they know using words and language. Judgments are made in the first three minutes of a job interview or meeting based on the hidden rules of language. Individuals who are unable to use the proper register may be passed over regardless of their ability or talents. There are people in the world who are very intelligent and have profound knowledge, ideas for inventions, cures for illnesses, and solutions to problems, but in order for them to communicate, share, or sell these intellectual concepts, they must be able to translate them into or represent them with words and language that others can understand.

Unique patterns of language (the words and how they are used) are observed in each of the economic classes. When an individual does not use the rules or language of a group, misunderstandings and assumptions about their ability or intelligence may occur. Schools use formal register on tests, in textbooks, and in classes. At work, technical manuals and instructions are written in formal register. In order to advance, individuals must be able to read, write, and speak using formal register. On the street, individuals must be able to read nonverbals and use and understand casual register. In the corporate world, not understanding one or two sentences in a contract can cost millions of dollars. Language is necessary to survive, communicate, and perform all kinds of tasks in any environment, from negotiating million-dollar contracts to mixing baby formula.

How you can use this information: Learn the five registers, story structure, and patterns of language, and understand when and how each pattern is used. A straight-to-the-point pattern of conversation at work or school saves time and gets the job done. This pattern is very different from the circular one used to talk with friends. Understanding these patterns and when and why they are used can help you avoid misunderstandings. Build personal resources by increasing the vocabulary at your command and your ability to negotiate and communicate. Language is a resource that will influence respect, relationships both personal and professional, and the ability to respond in any situation for an entire lifetime. Labels and words are the tools the mind uses to address situations and tasks; language is the resource the mind uses to speak thoughts and dreams into reality.

The Argument in Signs shows the importance of formal register, as well as nonverbals, and uses a story to illustrate mental models. Good storytellers weave experiences into designs and mind pictures that make connections with listeners. All learning is double coded; it takes place in both the emotion and the intellect. Stories show relationships and allow us to connect with the hero, characters, and historical or everyday events. They provide a structure to store information, role models, and patterns that can be used to find our own voice and way.

Kathleen Kuiper, editor of *Merriam-Webster's Encyclopedia of Literature,* describes language this way: "It is through the naming of objects, telling of stories, and singing of songs that we know ourselves and others. Whether trickster tales or nursery rhymes are the first things we remember hearing, we have learned to live our lives by means of narrative—the stories our mothers told us, the books our brothers and sisters read to us (and the volumes we chose to read to them), and the holy books and textbooks that we read and memorized as children and still recall with perfect clarity. By these means we develop, however weakly or strongly, our moral natures, we discover who we are and who we are not, what we would give anything to be, and precisely what we would be willing to sacrifice to gain the prize. We need stories and songs to live fully."

Do you have a favorite story?
Why is it your favorite?

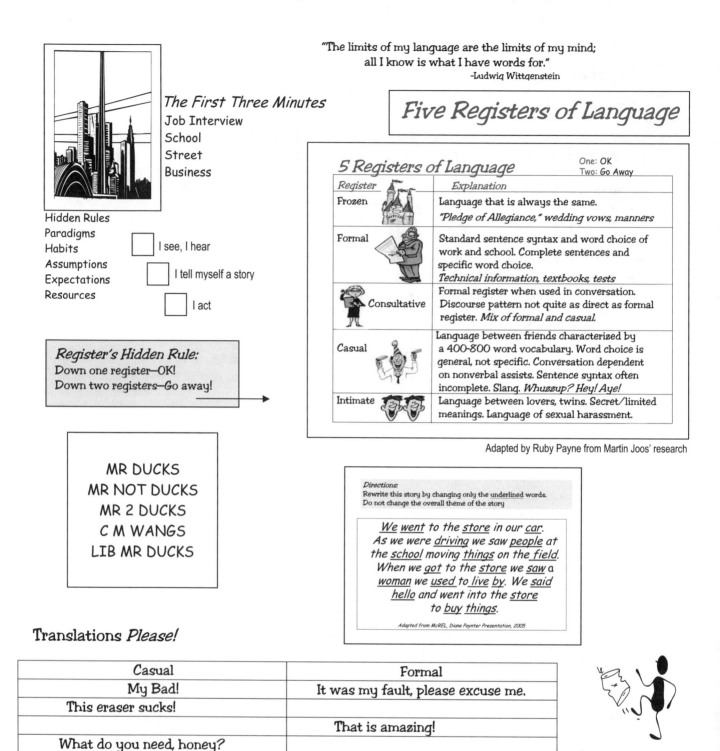

"The limits of my language are the limits of my mind; all I know is what I have words for."
-Ludwig Wittgenstein

The First Three Minutes
Job Interview
School
Street
Business

Hidden Rules
Paradigms
Habits
Assumptions
Expectations
Resources

☐ I see, I hear

☐ I tell myself a story

☐ I act

Register's Hidden Rule:
Down one register—OK!
Down two registers—Go away!

⟶

MR DUCKS
MR NOT DUCKS
MR 2 DUCKS
C M WANGS
LIB MR DUCKS

Five Registers of Language

5 Registers of Language

One: OK
Two: Go Away

Register		Explanation
Frozen		Language that is always the same. *"Pledge of Allegiance," wedding vows, manners*
Formal		Standard sentence syntax and word choice of work and school. Complete sentences and specific word choice. *Technical information, textbooks, tests*
Consultative		Formal register when used in conversation. Discourse pattern not quite as direct as formal register. *Mix of formal and casual.*
Casual		Language between friends characterized by a 400-800 word vocabulary. Word choice is general, not specific. Conversation dependent on nonverbal assists. Sentence syntax often incomplete. Slang. *Whuzzup? Hey! Aye!*
Intimate		Language between lovers, twins. Secret/limited meanings. Language of sexual harassment.

Adapted by Ruby Payne from Martin Joos' research

Directions:
Rewrite this story by changing only the underlined words.
Do not change the overall theme of the story

We went to the store in our car.
As we were driving we saw people at the school moving things on the field. When we got to the store we saw a woman we used to live by. We said hello and went into the store to buy things.

Adapted from McREL, Diane Paynter Presentation, 2005

Translations *Please!*

Casual	Formal
My Bad!	It was my fault, please excuse me.
This eraser sucks!	
	That is amazing!
What do you need, honey?	
	Oh my!

How do you say that in Standard American Formal English?

"I pledge allegiance to the flag of the United States of America and to the republic for which it stands, one nation, under God, indivisible, with liberty and justice for all."

_____

_____

_____

Directions
Reporting
Negotiation
Argument
Mediation
Communication
Self-Talk

240
NONVERBALS

The Luxury of Language

From *Meaningful Differences in the Everyday Experiences of Young American Children* by Betty Hart and Todd Risley

Working Vocabulary	Economic Class	Number of Words	Encouragements	Restrictions
1,200 for 36-month-old	Professional	30 Million	5	1
No information	Working	20 Million	2	1
900 for adult	Welfare	10 Million	1	2

WORKING VOCABULARY is the term used for the number of words actually used.

NUMBER OF WORDS refers to the number of words children living in stable households were exposed to from the ages of 6 months to 3 years. Research shows that the more words children hear from their parents (TV doesn't count) in the first three years, the more neuro-pathways are developed in the brain.

MEDIATION is a three-step process to teach what, why, and how. What: Get out of the street! Why: You might get hit by a car. How: Cross with an adult, look both ways, cross at the crosswalk. Mediation teaches and explains. R+R+R=R+R+R

ENCOURAGEMENTS are the number of time a child is encouraged by an adult to learn and explore.

RESTRICTIONS are the number of times a child is discouraged from this exploration or corrected.

BUILDING BLOCKS: Words are used to make connections to other words, mental images, and build a knowledge bank. For example, if a child knows the word *bird,* he or she can make connections by adding words for color and size, then add a name: bird, big, grey and orange, robin.

How could you use the
What, Why, and How process
to increase language and learning
for a young child?

Language of Self -Talk: Positive, Procedural, Mediation

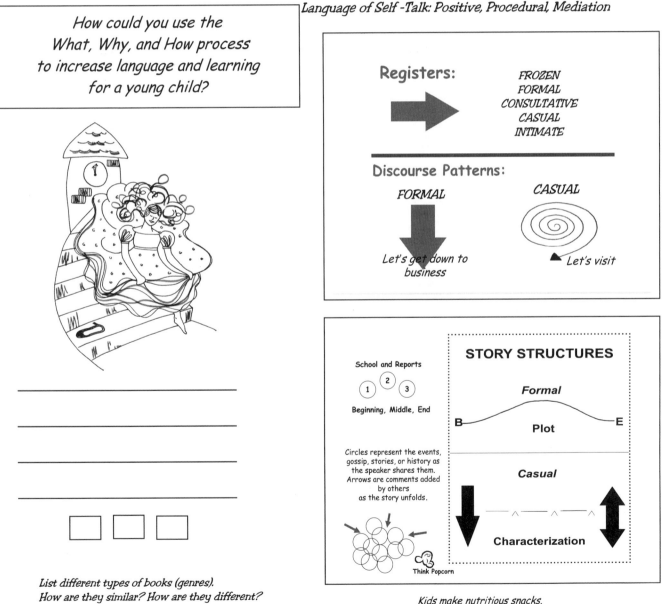

Registers:

FROZEN
FORMAL
CONSULTATIVE
CASUAL
INTIMATE

Discourse Patterns:

FORMAL

Let's get down to business

CASUAL

Let's visit

STORY STRUCTURES

School and Reports

① ②
  ③

Beginning, Middle, End

Circles represent the events, gossip, stories, or history as the speaker shares them.
Arrows are comments added by others as the story unfolds.

Think Popcorn

Formal

B ——— E

Plot

Casual

Characterization

_____

_____

_____

_____

▢ ▢ ▢

List different types of books (genres).
How are they similar? How are they different?

Kids make nutritious snacks.
Infant abducted from hospital safe.
Include your children when baking cookies.

Vocabulary Builders

To survive in poverty, individuals must have resources to use nonverbals and sensory information.
To survive at school and work, the ability to translate concrete or sensory information into abstract, verbal terms is needed.

> For a task to be done correctly, individuals must have:
> a plan, a procedure, vocabulary, labels, and a language.
> Words and labels are the tools of the mind.
> We need language to communicate and negotiate.

Declarative: the what, facts, concepts, information

Subject	Declarative	Procedural
Science		
Mathematics		
Geography		
Language Arts		
History		

According to Learner Centered Education, what *percentage* of each type of information is needed to master these subjects in school?
www.learnercentered.ed.org, Hal Robertson, 2005

The word, term, or concept

Textbook, Teacher, Standard Definition	In my words
• Formal register • Meets class requirements • Teacher or textbook words • Words that would appear on a test	• Any register • My own words • Stated so I understand
Mental Model	*Connections, Purpose, or Pattern*
• Sketch or drawing • Picture • Story • Analogy or metaphor • Pattern • Structure • Purpose	• Shows relationships • Connections to other classes, subject areas, or systems • Connections to experiences • Shows patterns or affinity • Metaphor • Analogy

Synonym   Antonym   Home language   Adapted from Diane Paynter

Language and Vocabulary Bank Account

Deposits	Withdrawals
Use language that is *hidden rule* appropriate	Move two registers lower during a conversation
Increase the number of words in your vocabulary	
Know the meaning of every word you use	Use words when you don't know their meanings
Use drawings and representations of words	Use casual register when formal register is required
Use frozen words: please, thank you, etc.	
Use million-dollar words	Use fifty-cent words or take out a language loan
Use the language of a content area, standard, or vocation	Use words such as *guess* for prediction, hypothesis, inquiry
Use games and reframes to help you learn vocabulary	Just try to remember
Develop language to negotiate and communicate	Use nonverbals, fight, leave it to fate

Deposits	Withdrawals

Procedural, the how and why, the steps, the translation

Procedural words:
select, identify, state, explain, retell, contrast, construct, apply, illustrate, analyze, compare, organize, create, design, develop, evaluate, justify, critique

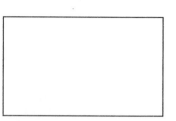

Johnny has three green apples and seven red apples.
Draw a table to compare the apples.

Build resources by playing games using:
Concepts
Categories
Classifications
Patterns
Answers
Sketches
Tasks

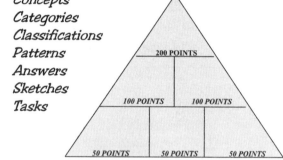

Every language has five registers.
Write words from every register for these:
Hobbies
Transportation
Personality traits
People   Chemistry
Food   Music
Medicine   Occupations
Animals

Increase your vocabulary by trading up ...
Increase the value of these one-dollar words:
Looked: peeked, glanced, inspected, viewed, examined, watched, spotted, observed
Asked:
Said:
Horse:
Laughed:
Car:

Three words that describe you:

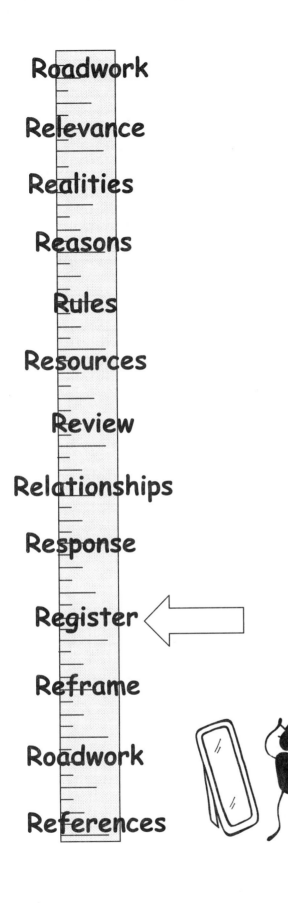

Roadwork

Relevance

Realities

Reasons

Rules

Resources

Review

Relationships

Response

Register ⬅

Reframe

Roadwork

References

What did you learn?
Why is it important?
How will you use this information?

Write it in casual or formal register:
a family tale
how you got your name
a story of your grandparents
a funny family story

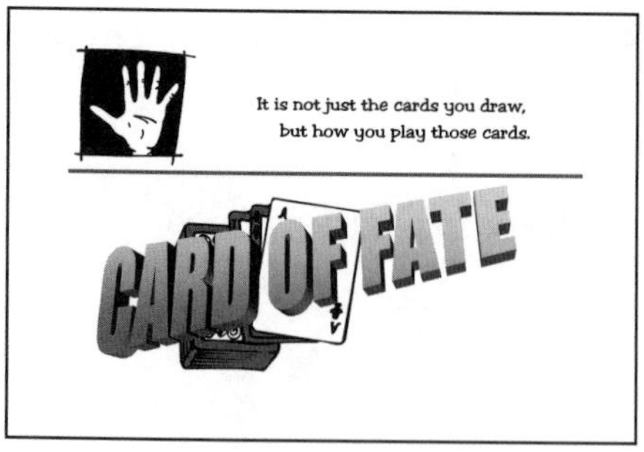

It is not just the cards you draw,
but how you play those cards.

CARD OF FATE

Use what you learned and a card of fate
to prepare for a job interview.

After the interview, complete a second
card of fate to determine next steps

What is the current situation?_____

What is the reality of the current situation?_____

_____

Is this important? Why or why not? _____

Do I need to respond? How long can I wait before I respond? How will I respond? _____

_____

What are possible actions, options, solutions?_____

_____

What resources are available? _____

What resources are missing? _____

Will a different resource work?_____

How can I get this resource?_____

What response will I try?_____

Why will this work?_____

Why won't it work?_____

How will I know it worked?_____

What else will I try if it doesn't work? Plan B:_____

_____

_____

_____

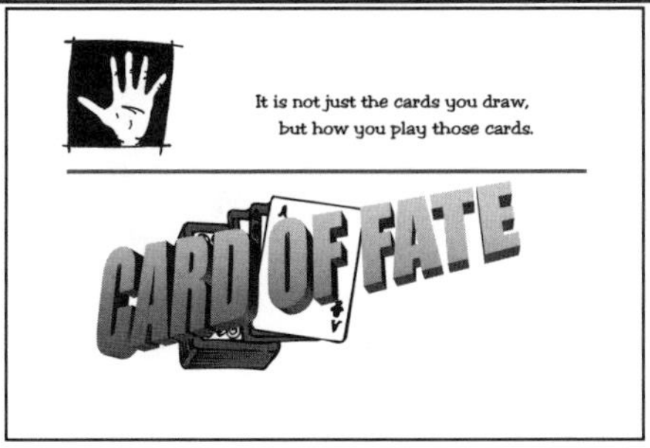

It is not just the cards you draw,
but how you play those cards.

CARD OF FATE

What is the current situation?_____

What is the reality of the current situation?_____

_____

Is this important? Why or why not? _____

Do I need to respond? How long can I wait before I respond? How will I respond? _____

_____

Possible actions, options, solutions?_____

_____

What resources are available? _____

What resources are missing? _____

Will a different resource work?_____

How can I get this resource?_____

What response will I try?_____

Why will this work?_____

Why won't it work?_____

How will I know it worked?_____

What else will I try if it doesn't work? Plan B:_____

_____

_____

_____

Chapter 11
REFRAME

"You cannot shake hands with a clenched fist."
-Indira Gandhi

What this is: *Reframe* is a term for translating information from one form into another. The mind continuously sorts information using patterns, paradigms, and connections to prior knowledge and experiences. Data is gathered using the five senses (sensory or concrete), and then translated or reframed into abstract information that can be used and stored in the mind. For learning to take place, information must be translated from its concrete form *outside* the head into an abstract form *inside* the head, *concrete to abstract*. Teaching takes place outside the head and is an external process; learning takes place inside the head and is an internal process.

Abstract representational systems, like the alphabet, are used to form words and labels that can be used to communicate the sensory information. An example: To say it is a hot day is using sensory data. To say it is 104° outside is using an abstract form, 104°, to represent sensory data about heat. This translation or reframe gives information a common value, measure, and language that can be communicated and understood.

A mental model is a picture, a story, a two-dimensional drawing, analogy, or metaphor. Mental models are used to hold information in the mind and show the pattern, structure, or purpose.

Why this is important: The mind can use a mental model to quickly sort and store information by relating to the pattern, purpose or structure. All humans have fundamental ways of processing information; these processes are the infrastructure of the mind. They are *input, elaboration, and output.*

- Input is the gathering of information, the basic learning, the what.
- Elaboration occurs when the information is sorted based upon the why in order to be used.
- Output is how the information is communicated back in relation to daily life and surroundings—the how.

When information is reframed, it is translated into a form that has a relationship or meaning that can be remembered easily, can be used, and can help individuals learn faster and remember longer.

How you can use this information: Understand how abstract representations affect learning. Use mental models and develop learning strategies, skills, resources, and processes to help sort and learn. Use strategies such as question making, sketching, humor, and graphic organizers, and look for the pattern, structure, or purpose of information as it relates to the subject or your life.

When Stump Barnes lost his leg, he had to reframe his dream; he had to see himself in his future picture differently than when it was first developed. Reframe how you see yourself now into a future picture of what you want to be and do, then work toward it.

Fact: Each year, hundreds of thousands of young adults leave school without successfully completing a high school program.

Reframe: "Every single school day, 180 school buses drive out of America's schoolyards filled with students who will not return."

-Franklin Schargel, *Dropout Prevention Tools*

Reprinted with pemission of Timothy Lucas

Three Reframes for Learning about Learning
Input, Elaboration, Output

What, Why, How

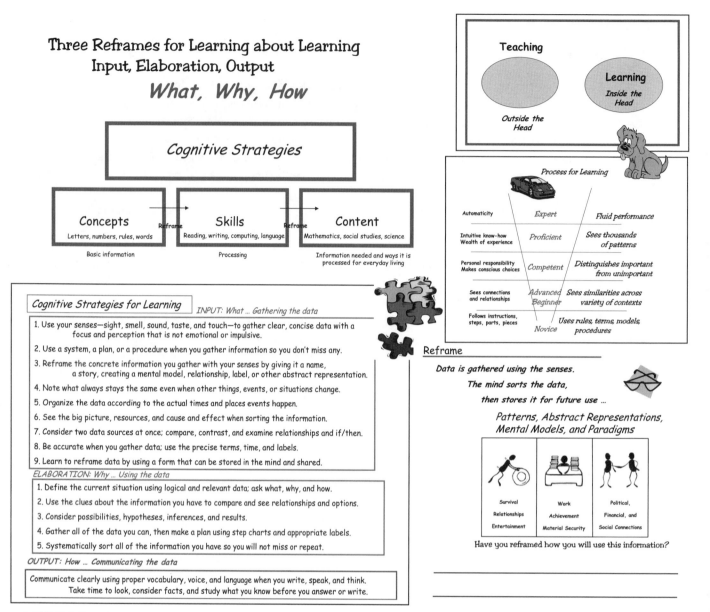

Cognitive Strategies

Concepts — *Reframe* → Skills — *Reframe* → Content

Concepts
Letters, numbers, rules, words
Basic information

Skills
Reading, writing, computing, language
Processing

Content
Mathematics, social studies, science
Information needed and ways it is processed for everyday living

Teaching — *Outside the Head*
Learning — *Inside the Head*

Process for Learning

Automaticity	*Expert*	Fluid performance
Intuitive know-how Wealth of experience	*Proficient*	Sees thousands of patterns
Personal responsibility Makes conscious choices	*Competent*	Distinguishes important from unimportant
Sees connections and relationships	*Advanced Beginner*	Sees similarities across variety of contexts
Follows instructions, steps, parts, pieces	*Novice*	Uses rules, terms, models, procedures

Cognitive Strategies for Learning   *INPUT: What ... Gathering the data*

1. Use your senses—sight, smell, sound, taste, and touch—to gather clear, concise data with a focus and perception that is not emotional or impulsive.
2. Use a system, a plan, or a procedure when you gather information so you don't miss any.
3. Reframe the concrete information you gather with your senses by giving it a name, a story, creating a mental model, relationship, label, or other abstract representation.
4. Note what always stays the same even when other things, events, or situations change.
5. Organize the data according to the actual times and places events happen.
6. See the big picture, resources, and cause and effect when sorting the information.
7. Consider two data sources at once; compare, contrast, and examine relationships and if/then.
8. Be accurate when you gather data; use the precise terms, time, and labels.
9. Learn to reframe data by using a form that can be stored in the mind and shared.

ELABORATION: Why ... Using the data

1. Define the current situation using logical and relevant data; ask what, why, and how.
2. Use the clues about the information you have to compare and see relationships and options.
3. Consider possibilities, hypotheses, inferences, and results.
4. Gather all of the data you can, then make a plan using step charts and appropriate labels.
5. Systematically sort all of the information you have so you will not miss or repeat.

OUTPUT: How ... Communicating the data

Communicate clearly using proper vocabulary, voice, and language when you write, speak, and think.
Take time to look, consider facts, and study what you know before you answer or write.

Reframe

Data is gathered using the senses.

The mind sorts the data,

then stores it for future use ...

Patterns, Abstract Representations, Mental Models, and Paradigms

Survival
Relationships
Entertainment

Work
Achievement
Material Security

Political,
Financial, and
Social Connections

Have you reframed how you will use this information?

Sensory Data Is Reframed to Abstract Data

Reframe how you view intelligence

Word Smart

Logic Smart   ← Define these terms at
1. Work

Self Smart
2. Street

People Smart
3. School

Picture Smart

Music Smart   *Use 1, 2, or 3, to rate each intelligence according to where would be of most value.*

Body Smart

Nature Smart   *From Dropout Prevention Tools Franklin P. Schargel, 2002*

Concrete or Sensory	Abstract: School and Work
	Bank Account
Weather, Sickness	Temperature in Degrees
Intelligence	
	Deed or Title
	Photograph
A Long Way	
	SMART Goal in Writing
	Diploma
	Hours and Minutes
A Person	

Mental models: a story, picture, metaphor, analogy, two-dimensional drawing
Reframes: cartoons, representation, graphic organizer

Space Needed for Math
Use space words: right, left, front, below, beside, over, under, north, south, east, west.
What stays the same? What changes?

On which side of the tip of the arrow is the dot?

+ + + + + +
Good Guys

- - - - - - -
Bad Guys

Mental model for multiplication of positive and negative numbers.

Good Guy (+)	Comes to Town (+)	Get (=)
Bad Guy (-)	Leaves Town (+)	Get (=)
+	+	+
+	-	-
-	+	-
-	-	?

La Marcha

The Elephant in the Room

"Two roads diverged,
in a wood, and I
Took the one least traveled by,
And it has made all the difference." –Robert Frost

!?.

WHAT: *Mental models are the internalized, mental representations of things in the world, the internal symbols or representations a person uses to understand, sort, and use information.*

Mental models are how the mind holds abstract information that has no sensory representation.

WHY: *Mental models show patterns, structures, or the purpose.*

HOW: *Use mental models for space, time, decoding, part to whole, formal register, and to sort what is important from what is not.*

Life is a journey ...

Draw it or write it, put in a safe place, check progress daily, revise.
Planning Backwards

Part to Whole

data folders
transcripts
action plans

Plan and Label

1,2,3,4 Topic	Topic
Topic	Topic
Paragraph	References

Steps	Time
1.	
2.	
3.	
4.	
5.	

Planning and Sorting Time:

Covey's big rock method

the juggler

the timeline

the step chart

past, present, and future

Reframe how you study ...

What is your *primary* learning style?
Do you learn and retain information better if you ...

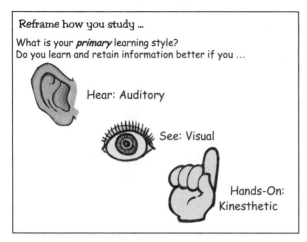

Hear: Auditory

See: Visual

Hands-On: Kinesthetic

What's your style?

How do you complete tasks?

Sequential or Random

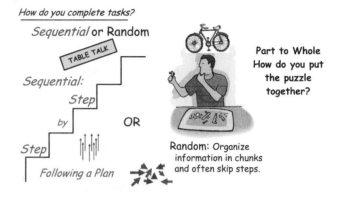

TABLE TALK

Sequential:

Step

by

OR

Step

Following a Plan

Part to Whole
How do you put the puzzle together?

Random: Organize information in chunks and often skip steps.

Use a cartoon to develop a beginning, middle, and end for your story.

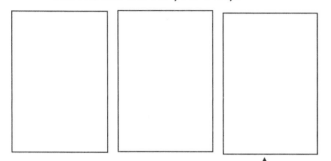

Outline or reframe a chapter ↑

Personal Reframes

How you talk to yourself, the voice and language of self-talk, may require a reframe. When individuals lack the adult voice, their self-talk will be very discouraging. Use the adult voice and the positive parent voice to support your efforts. Every physical creation is preceded by a mental picture—"Believing is seeing."

Self-talk can be an affirmation, steps through a task, a plan, the to-do list, or can connect you to voices from the past. *If the self-talk you use is not a resource ... REFRAME IT!*

Reframe behavior...

1. What did you do?
2. When you did that, what did you want?
3. List four other things you could have done.
4. What will you do next time?

Self-talk: Do you need a REFRAME?

Child   *Parent*   *Adult*

Procedural

Future picture

Good job!

If you choose ... then you have chosen.

The stories I tell myself.

ME

Question:

_____

_____

_____

_____

Four Answers: A B C D
Three Rules:

1. One wrong answer choice must be funny.
2. Only one answer choice may be right.
3. May not use "all of the above" or "none of the above."

Sketchers
Onomatopoeia
Degrees
Celebrate
Hope
Love
Family
License
Marriage
Hypothesis

Roadwork

Relevance

Reasons

Realities

Rules

Resources

Review

Relationships

Response

Register

Reframe

Roadwork

References

What did you learn?
Why is it important?
How will you use this information?

Ten Ways to Reframe
1. Use mental models and create your own.
2. Develop systems and patterns to sort information.
3. Set goals and use graphic organizers and planners.
4. Use procedural and positive self-talk.
5. Translate information from one form or register into another.
6. Change abstract words or concepts into actions.
7. Develop and use rubrics.
8. Learn language patterns, then develop automaticity
9. Make questions.
10. Cartoon, sketch, or draw what is important to summarize.

It is not just the cards you draw,
but how you play those cards.

CARD OF FATE

Juan is an excellent welder, but does not read or use written plans well. He has been offered a promotion to the position of foreman. This job will require a lot of paperwork, but it will pay $8.00 more per hour than Juan makes now.

What is the current situation?_____

What is the reality of the current situation?_____

_____

Is this important? Why or why not?_____

Do I need to respond? How long can I wait before I respond? How will I respond?_____

_____

 What are possible actions, options, solutions?_____

_____

What resources are available?_____

What resources are missing?_____

Will a different resource work?_____

How can I get this resource?_____

_____

What response will I try?_____

Why will this work?_____

Why won't this work?_____

How will I know it worked?_____

What else will I try if it doesn't work? Plan B:_____

Notes

Chapter 12
ROADWORK

"Begin with the end in mind."
-Stephen Covey

What this is: Life is a journey and every day is a road trip. Each new trip requires knowing where you want to go, what you want to do, and how you want to finish. Knowing the destination, goal, or future picture is necessary to chart and stay on course.

Why this is important: Have you ever been so busy driving you forgot to get gas? The resources available to individuals, systems, people, and situations constantly change. To stay on track, take time to "reflect and review"; see patterns, realities, and resources; be aware and "awake," and always consider why, as well as what and how. The ability to understand why something is occurring and knowing and keeping purpose or vision in mind will support reframes and responses that move you toward the desired goal or future picture and help avoid wrong turns or detours.

How you can use this information: Develop personal habits, resources, and a future picture. Decide what is important, and identify role models and beliefs that will remain constant when the rules of the road change. Read the patterns; manage time and develop self-talk and relationships that encourage and inspire. Increase awareness and knowledge about yourself, your community, and the world. Seek wisdom, as well as information—they are not the same thing, and both are needed. Respect education, formal and informal, and honor intelligence and resources, especially those that are different from your own. Use what you know and your unique gifts to chart your own course and make a positive difference for yourself and others. As Mahatma Gandhi said, "Be the change you wish to see in the world."

My Favorite Quote(s):

What do you want to be? Begin now ...
What do you want to do? Do it now ...
What do you want to have? Why ...

Your mind is a tool, a resource, a weapon ...

My Board of Directors:
Who do I look to, talk to, listen to, learn from ...
1.
2.
3.
4.
5.
6.
7.
8.
9.
10.

Our answers are as only good as the questions we ask ...
What are you asking?
What is your job?
What is your work?
What is important?
Who do you listen to?
Always ask why ...
My non-negotiables are:

If I choose ... then I have chosen ...
If I choose ... then I chose ...

Walk a mile in these shoes:

John lives in foster care.
When he is 18 he will age out.
He is 14 now.
Write a SMART Goal and
a SMART Action Plan for John
that will let him be independent
when he turns 18.

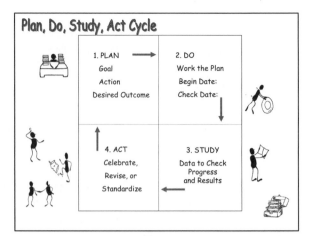

Plan, Do, Study, Act Cycle

1. PLAN Goal Action Desired Outcome	2. DO Work the Plan Begin Date: Check Date:
4. ACT Celebrate, Revise, or Standardize	3. STUDY Data to Check Progress and Results

The PDSA Cycle ... Plan it; do it; study results.
Celebrate, wait, or revise the plan.
Plan, do it, study results, celebrate, wait, revise the plan.
Plan, do, study the results ...
Always consider resources and information.
Keep getting better. Good is the enemy of great.

"If our circumstances are going to change,
we must take the brush of faith
and paint in vibrant living color on the canvas of our tomorrow."
—Bishop J.W. Macklin

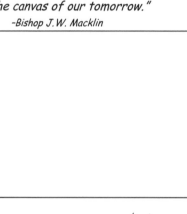

Keep drawing today ...
and the tomorrow you want to live in.
Erase mistakes with forgiveness and new starts.
Use brushstrokes of hope
and colors of respect, wisdom, and knowledge.

Dreams are travels for the soul.
Where will you travel?
Every journey begins
with a single step ...

Use self-talk, promise statements,
photos, quotations, songs, books, poetry,
and role models to inspire and encourage.
Build your own resource list.

I Promise Myself ...
to stay strong
to respect myself and others
to use my resources and talents to make a difference
to look for possibilities and see options
to work to make my dreams come true
to forget the mistakes of the past and
press on to the accomplishments of my future
to smile and find humor
to listen to stories different than my own
to control the things I can
to forgive myself for the things I cannot
to care
to choose my way and use my unique voice
to remember I can
to hope
to dream
to ...

Use Positive Self-Talk: The Personal Language

Every day in every way I am getting better.
I am responsible for my success.
I can control my actions and my emotions.
I can do more with a good education.
I am grateful for ...
I care about _____ and _____ cares about me.
If I can do _____, then I can do _____.
I have good resources.
It is funny that ...
I am good at ...
I choose.
I have faith.
I have a choice.

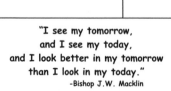

"I see my tomorrow,
and I see my today,
and I look better in my tomorrow
than I look in my today."
—Bishop J.W. Macklin

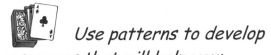 *Use patterns to develop resources that will help you:*

- *be in control*
- *be respected*
- *be smarter*
- *play the hands you get*
- *win more often*
- *predict and plan*
- *see options*
- *change things that need to be changed*
- *keep from being cheated*
- *get what you want*
- *be safe*
- *make the difference that only you can make*

"Too often we are scared.
Scared of what we might not be able to do.
Scared of what people might think if we tried.
We let our fears stand in the way of our hopes.
Why?"   -Barry Sanders

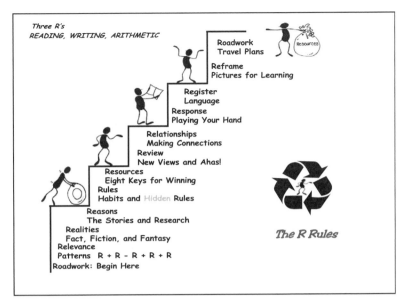

Rules + Rigor + Relationships = Resources + Results + Respect

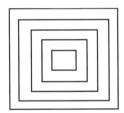

What are you a part of?

The R Rules is about patterns and relationships.
The what, why, and how
of rules, realities, and resources.
I hope *The R Rules* helped you learn about yourself,
who you are, and who you want to be.
I hope you are inspired to keep learning
and to operate from a place of hope
rather than a place of resignation.
I hope you will see possibilities where you once accepted limits.
I hope you will ask why, and then why not.
I hope you will share what you learn with others
so they, too, will have choices.
I hope you will not play small,
but instead show your unique talents and skills,
and by doing so
give others permission to do the same.
I hope you will use your mind as a tool
to invent and discover.
I hope you will use your mind as a weapon
to fight injustice and fear.
I hope you will use your resources to create
the future that you and I want to live in.
I hope you will know the excitement and promise
that only a person beginning a long journey
whose destination is seen
yet uncertain can know.
I hope you will have courage to take new roads.
I hope you will follow your dreams.
I hope.

Reference Section

Quotations
Resource Project
Tools
R Rules Definitions
Bibliography

Quotations

We learn by using role models, observing the ways people behave, their beliefs, their dreams, their purpose.
Keeping a journal of quotations is a way to learn from and connect with other people.
Use their voices as a resource to inspire and direct your own.

R + R – R = R + R -Grant East
Rules + Regulations – Relationships = Resentment + Rebellion

R + R + R = R + R + R   -Betti Souther

Rules + Regulations + Relationships = Resources + Resiliency + Respect

Rules + Rigor + Relationships = Resources + Results + Respect

"No one can make you feel inferior unless you give them license." -Eleanor Roosevelt

"It is not that I am so smart,
I just stay with a problem longer than most." –Albert Einstein

"A true leader has the confidence to stand alone, the courage to make tough decisions,
and the compassion to listen to the needs of others. He does not set out to be a leader,
but becomes one by the quality of his actions and the integrity of his intent.
In the end, leaders are much like eagles ...
they don't flock; you find them one at a time."   -unknown

"Even a blind squirrel finds an acorn every once in a while." -unknown

"To decide what is enough, first determine what will be too much."
-unknown

"Good is the enemy of great."   –Jim Collins

"Deep speaks to deep." –unknown

"A person wrapped up in himself makes a very small package."   -J.W. Macklin

*"Service is the rent we pay
for the privilege of living in this world."*
–N. Eldon Tanner

"Accumulate learning by study,
understand what you learn by questioning." –Cha'n Master Mingjiao

"If we all did the things we are capable of doing, we would literally astound ourselves."
-Thomas Edison

"I see my tomorrow, and I see my today,
and I look better in my tomorrow than I look in my today."
–Bishop J.W. Macklin

"What is worse than being blind
is having the ability to see and
not having a vision."
-Helen Keller

"Sometimes not getting what you want is a good thing.
Sometimes silence is the best answer." -unknown

"Learn the rules so you know how to break them properly." -unknown

"I trust that everything happens for a reason,
even when we're not wise enough to see it."
-Oprah Winfrey

"The world has improved mostly because of unorthodox people doing unorthodox things.
Not surprisingly, they had the courage and daring to think that they could make a difference." – Ruby Dee

"We must be big enough to let somebody else be big." -Bishop J.W. Macklin

"We must be the change we wish to see
in the world." –Mahatma Gandhi

"The more we can see people in terms of their unseen potential, the more we can use our imagination rather than
our memory, with our spouses, our children, our co-workers and our employees." -Stephen Covey

"Faith is daring to put your dreams to the
test. It is better to try to do something and fail
than to try to do nothing and succeed."
–Robert Schuller

"Learning happens inside the head.
Teaching happens outside the head."
–Ruby Payne

"You cannot wake a person who is pretending to be asleep." -Navajo proverb

He is a ~~wealthy~~ man who is courageous.
He is a ~~middle class~~ man who is courageous.
He is a ~~poor~~ man who is courageous.
He is a courageous man.

"The first requisite for success is the ability to
apply your physical and mental energies to one
problem incessantly without growing weary."
–Thomas Edison

"Real joy comes not from ease or riches or from the praise of men,
but from doing something worthwhile." —Wilfred T. Grenfell

"It's not what happens to you,
it is what you do about it."
–W. Mitchell

"The message I stress: To make it stop, study your lessons.
Don't settle for less; even the genius asks questions …
The power is in the people and politics we address."
–Tupac Shakur

"Insanity is doing the same thing
over and over again
and expecting a different result."
–Albert Einstein

"The elders understood the wisdom of solitude and quiet,
a time for man's spirit to bathe in the solace of spiritual strength."
–Howard Rainer

"Litigation is a costly substitute for integrity." –unknown

"You can't legislate good will—that comes through education." –Malcom X

"Even if you are on the right track, you will get run over if you just sit there." –Will Rogers

"You see things
and you say, 'Why?'
I dream things that never were
and say, 'Why not?'"
–George Bernard Shaw

"We must not cease from exploration
and the end of our exploration
will be to arrive where we began
and know the place for the first time."
–t.s. eliot

Hope is…

Believing is seeing.

"Can we involve the expertise and experience of everyone in the organization?
We can't ignore the question. We've got to figure out how we can avoid the temptation
to design things for people instead of engaging them in creating their own response to change."
–Margaret Wheatley

"From this hour I ordain myself,
loos'd of limits and imaginary lines."
–Walt Whitman

"How wonderful it is that nobody need wait a single moment before beginning to improve the world."
-Anne Frank

"Change is good or bad depending on who owns the pocket it is in."
–unknown

"Two people I'm afraid of messin' up with: God and my mama, and not in that order."
–NFL player during an interview

"Commitment is the day-to-day work that turns visions into reality." –unknown

"Meaning is not something you stumble across, like the answer to a riddle or the prize in a treasure hunt.
Meaning is something you build into your life.
You build it out of your own past, out of your affections and loyalties,
out of the experience of humankind as it is passed on to you,
out of your own talent and understanding,
out of the things you believe in, out of the things and people you love,
out of the values for which you are willing to sacrifice something.
The ingredients are there.
You are the only one who can put them into that pattern that will be your life.
Let it be a life that has dignity and meaning for *you*.
If it doesn't then the particular balance of success and failure is of less account."
–John Gardner

"If you have come to help me, you can go home again.
But if you see my struggle as a part of your own survival, then perhaps we can work together."
-Lila Watson

"How are the children?"
–traditional greeting of the Masai tribe

"The role of the educator or social worker is not to save the individual,
but rather to offer a support system, role models, and opportunities to learn
that will increase the likelihood of the person's success.
Ultimately, the choice always belongs to the individual."
-Ruby Payne

"If individuals and organizations operate from the generative orientation,
from possiblity rather than resignation,
we can create the future into which we are living,
as opposed to merely reacting to it when we get there."
-Joe Jaworski

*"As we let our own light shine,
we unconsciously give others permission to do the same,
and we are liberated from our fear."*
–Marianne Williamson

I hope ...

Resources

Alateen: www.al-anon.alateen.org
America's Promise Alliance: www.americaspromise.org
American Red Cross: http://www.redcross.org
Assets: www.search-institute.org
Careers: www.careerkey.com and www.monster.com
        www.salary.com and www.salaryexpert.com
Career paths: www.careerclusters.org
        www.careervoyages.gov and www.dodea.edu
Child labor laws, work permits, hours, age, wages: www.dol.gov/dol/topic/youthlabor/
College and post-secondary: www.collegeispossible.org
        www.ed.gov/pubs/Prepare/pt1.html
        www.ed.gov/pubs/GettingReadyCollegeEarly/index.html
        http://www.ribghe.org/courseshs.htm
Credit and credit cards: www.practicalmoneyskills.com/English/index.php
        www.visa.ca/moneyskills/students
Department of Labor: www.dol.gov and www.federaljobsearch.com
Domestic violence: (800) 799-SAFE
Dropout and employment: www.focusas.com/Dropouts.html
Drug free: www.drugfreeamerica.org
Family and youth services: www.acf.hhs.gov/programs/fysb/
Family services by state: www.focusas.com
Financial assistance for education: www.nasfaa.org
        Vocational/technical school: www.vocational-technical-schools.com
        College: www.finaid.org/
Food stamps: www.fns.usda.gov/fsp/
Getting your first driver's license: www.dmv.org/
Green card: http://uscis.gov/graphics/1GreenCard.htm
Healthcare: AIDS hotline: (800) 342-2437
        Hepatitis hotline: (800) 390-1202
        National Rural Health Association: http://www.nrharural.org
        National Suicide Prevention Hotline: (800) SUICIDE
Healthcare for the homeless: www.nhchc.org
Interview skills: www.career.fsu.edu/employment/interview-guide.html
Immigration: www.uscis.gov/
Jobs and labor stats: www.bls.gov
Job shadowing: www.jobshadowing.org
Junior Achievement: www.ja.org
Learning disability testing and rights: www.iser.com/index.shtml
Learning styles: www.ncsu.edu/felder-public/Learning_Styles.html
Learning style survey online: www.ncsu.edu/felder-public/ILSdir/ilsweb.html
Medicare: www.medicare.gov
Money management: www.oprah.com/money/debtdiet/money_debtdiet_main.jhtml
Planned Parenthood: www.plannedparenthood.org
Prescription assistance: https://www.pparx.org/Intro.php
Runaway hotline: www.1800runaway.org/ (800) RUNAWAY
Salvation Army: www.salvationarmy.org/
Social Security: www.ssa.gov/
Tattoo removal: http://people.howstuffworks.com/tattoo-removal.htm and http://patient-info.com/tattoo.htm
Teen jobs: http://jobsearch.about.com/cs/justforstudents/a/teenjobs.htm
Teen pregnancy: www.teenpregnancy.org/resources
Voting rights: www.usdoj.gov/crt/voting/intro/intro.htm
WIC: www.fns.usda.gov/wic/
Young adults in jail or prison: www.childtrendsdatabank.org/indicators/89youngadultsJailPrison.cfm
Voter registration: www.civicyouth.org and www.lwv.org
        www.eac.gov/voter/Register%20to%20Vote and www.youthvote.org

Review the list of resources. Working as a team, review the mental models you created in the Realities section showing resources in your community. Discuss the chart on page 48 showing the four areas of research. List under the plus (+) the benefits of this list, under the delta (Δ) what you would change or add. Then create a plan (Rx) and work as a team to improve the list. Check resources that are available, and seek resources that are needed. Use the tables below to list additional categories, resources, and steps to improve the list.

Resources I will be responsible for getting information on:

What	When: Begin and end times	Who, where, and how

E-mail new resource listings to:

In addition, please include the following information: name of contact person, school or organization, phone number.

Tools

Processes to gather, translate, or reframe information.

- Mental models
- Abstract representational systems
- Strategies for document, technological, and quantitative literacy
- Learning processes for inquiry, identification, analysis, and response
- Identify patterns, predict, and plan
- Processes to discuss issues and systems, not people
- Part to whole
- Procedural task steps

Affinity Diagram

A process to gather ideas and classify, categorize, organize, and identify similarities, differences, and patterns.

Step 1: Write or state a question, item, characteristic, or issue.
Step 2: Silently or verbally brainstorm ideas related to the item or issue.
Step 3: Record each idea on a different sticky note.
Step 4: Sort ideas by putting items that have a connection together.
Step 5: For each group, select a title to describe the category or classification.

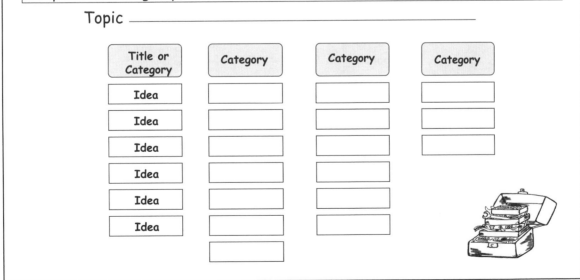

Topic _____

Title or Category	Category	Category	Category
Idea			
Idea			
Idea			
Idea			
Idea			
Idea			

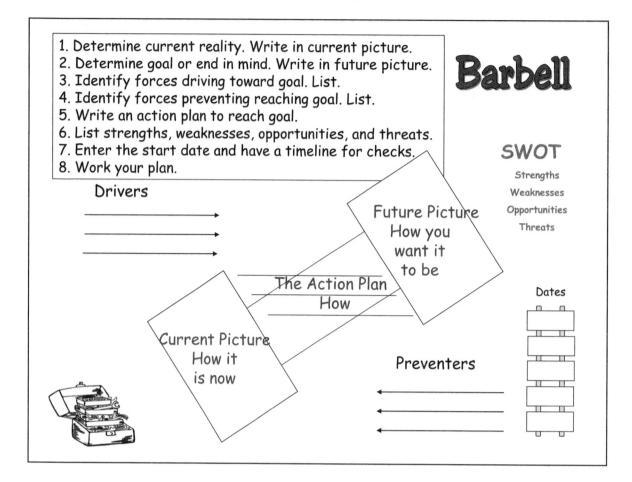

1. Determine current reality. Write in current picture.
2. Determine goal or end in mind. Write in future picture.
3. Identify forces driving toward goal. List.
4. Identify forces preventing reaching goal. List.
5. Write an action plan to reach goal.
6. List strengths, weaknesses, opportunities, and threats.
7. Enter the start date and have a timeline for checks.
8. Work your plan.

Barbell

Drivers

SWOT

Strengths
Weaknesses
Opportunities
Threats

Future Picture
How you
want it
to be

The Action Plan
How

Current Picture
How it
is now

Dates

Preventers

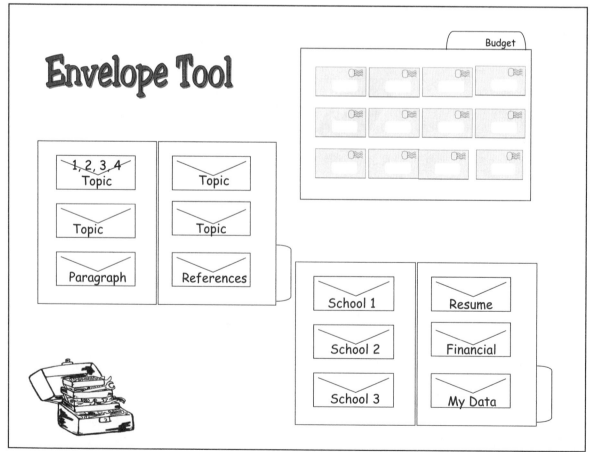

Envelope Tool

Budget

1, 2, 3, 4
Topic

Topic

Topic

Topic

Paragraph

References

School 1

Resume

School 2

Financial

School 3

My Data

Five Whys

Define the Current Situation

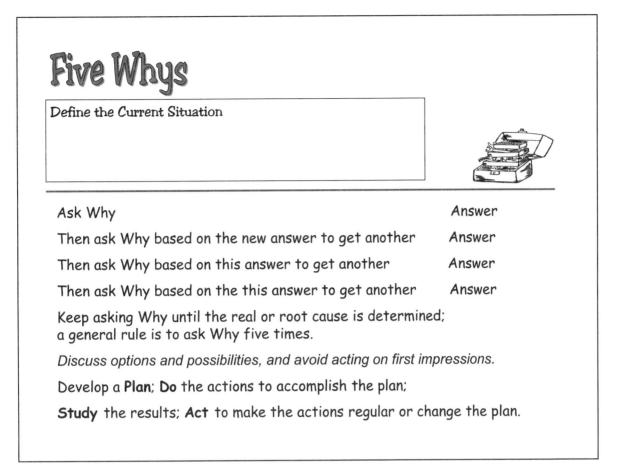

Ask Why	Answer
Then ask Why based on the new answer to get another	Answer
Then ask Why based on this answer to get another	Answer
Then ask Why based on the this answer to get another	Answer

Keep asking Why until the real or root cause is determined;
a general rule is to ask Why five times.

Discuss options and possibilities, and avoid acting on first impressions.

Develop a **Plan**; **Do** the actions to accomplish the plan;

Study the results; **Act** to make the actions regular or change the plan.

Force Field

A process to identify forces and patterns that drive or support an effort or restrain and work as barriers.

Step 1: Write the topic, subject, situation, or goal.
Step 2: List the reasons or forces moving toward a goal or action.
Step 3: List the reasons or forces that will be barriers to the action or goal.
Step 4: Select the forces that will help most, and then prioritize them.
Step 5: Prioritize the barriers.
Step 6: Change or eliminate the barriers; use the drivers to help reach the goal.

Topic: _____

Drivers ⟶	⟵ Barriers
1.	1.
2.	2.
3.	3.
4.	4.
5.	5.
6.	6.

If/Then

A tool for seeing patterns and choices, summarizing, and showing relationships, patterns, cause, and effect.

Step 1: IF   Write the topic, problem, plan, facts, prediction, hypothesis, event, cause, or action.
Step 2: THEN   Write what happened next, new prediction, solution, result, or next step.
Step 3: REPEAT Five rounds or to the end of the story or problem. Discuss options and possibilities; look for patterns.

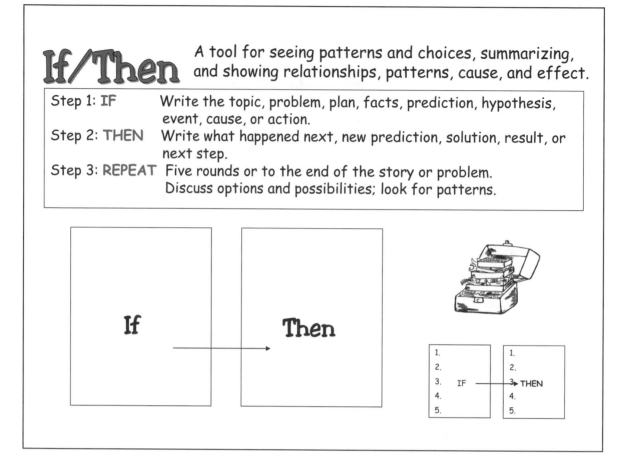

Lotus Diagram

Tool to show part to whole and sort, gather, and expand information and items related to a topic or event.

Step 1: Pick a topic and write it in the middle square.
Step 2: In each box surrounding the topic, list one related item.
Step 3: Each related item becomes the topic of a new lotus diagram.
Step 4: The related item goes in the center of the new lotus as a new topic.
Step 5: List in each surrounding box categories related to the new topic.
Step 6: Continue steps 3, 4, and 5 until you have explored all categories.

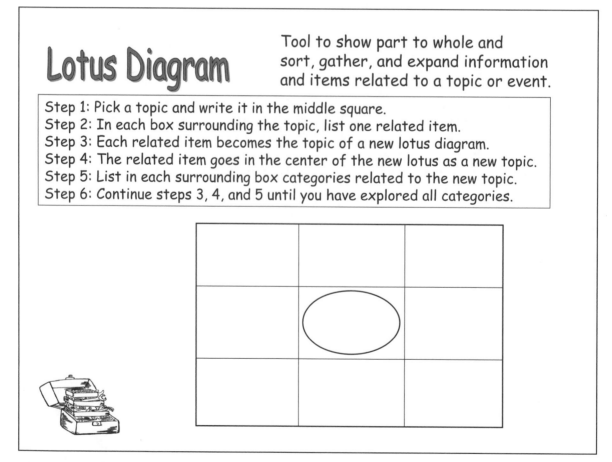

Lotus Diagram

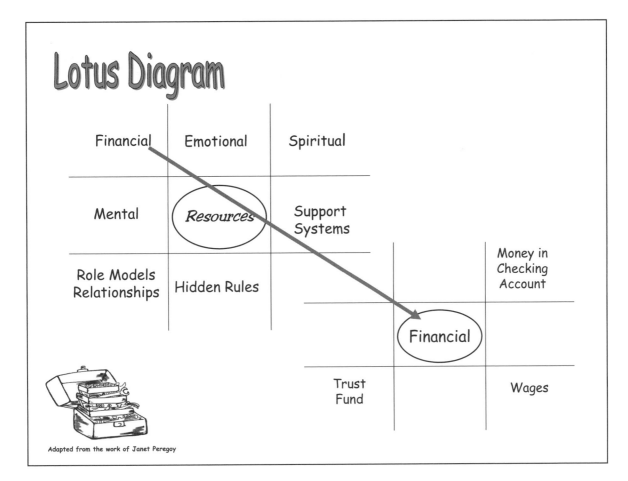

Financial	Emotional	Spiritual
Mental	*Resources*	Support Systems
Role Models Relationships	Hidden Rules	

	Money in Checking Account
Financial	
Trust Fund	Wages

Adapted from the work of Janet Peregoy

Plan, Do, Study, Act Cycle

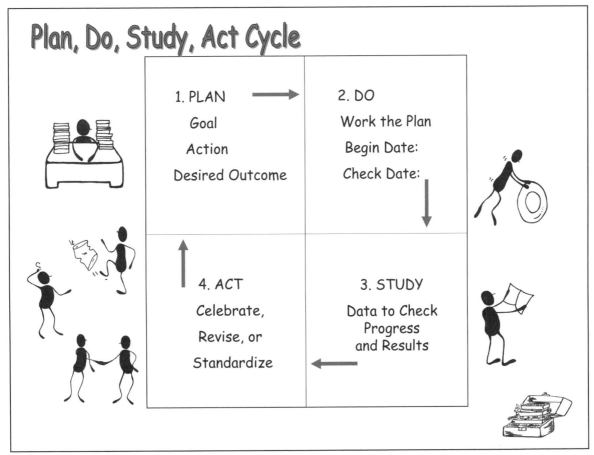

1. PLAN	2. DO
Goal	Work the Plan
Action	Begin Date:
Desired Outcome	Check Date:
4. ACT	3. STUDY
Celebrate,	Data to Check
Revise, or	Progress
Standardize	and Results

Planning Backward

A tool to start with the outcome or future picture, break it into parts, and develop action steps.

Step 1: State the desired end, goal, or future picture.
Step 2: List the end date or product in the last column on the right.
Step 3: In each section or column list what actions or steps will be taken to accomplish or reach the goal or outcome.
Step 4: Monitor progress and adjust as needed.

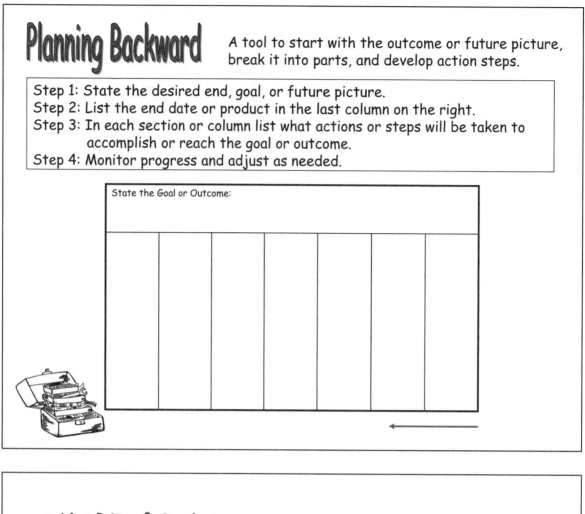

State the Goal or Outcome:

SMART GOALS

The parts of a goal are:
what, who, why, how, and when

SMART Goals are:
Specific, can be *Measured*, have an *Action, Results,* and a *Timeline.*

Specific	Measurement	Actions	Results	Timeline
Who will do what? **What** is the goal or desired outcome?	**Measure** Why are you doing this? What specifically will be improved or accomplished?	**How** List a strategy. Develop an action plan with steps.	**Consider** Future Picture Realistic Relevant Resources	**When** Goal will be accomplished or End time

SMART GOALS

The parts of a goal are:
what, who, why, how, and when

SMART Goals are:
Specific, can be *Measured*, have an *Action, Results,* and a *Timeline.*

Specific	Measurement	Actions	Results	Timeline
Who will do what? **What** is the goal or desired outcome?	**Measure** Why are you doing this? What specifically will be improved or accomplished?	**How** List a strategy. Develop an action plan with steps.	**Consider** Future Picture Realistic Relevant Resources	**When** Goal will be accomplished or End time

SMART ACTION PLAN

Action Plan

What	Who	When	How

↓ *In more detail ...*

Strategy Strategies	Measurement	Actions	Responsible Resources	Timeline
What will be done? List each strategy separately.	**Data** Beginning measure Progress measure End measure How will you know you met your goal?	**How** Steps that will be followed to accomplish strategy: 1, 2, 3, 4	**Who** is responsible for each step? What resources are needed?	**When** Will each action strategy be done: Start Date Checkpoints Progress Checks Completion Date

Spider Diagram

A tool to show part to whole and connections and expand information.

Step 1: List under the plus side things that are going well, working, having a positive impact, or you helping reach a goal.
Step 2: List under the delta side anything that could be changed to improve.
Step 3: Write a plan to improve or change using the items on the delta side.

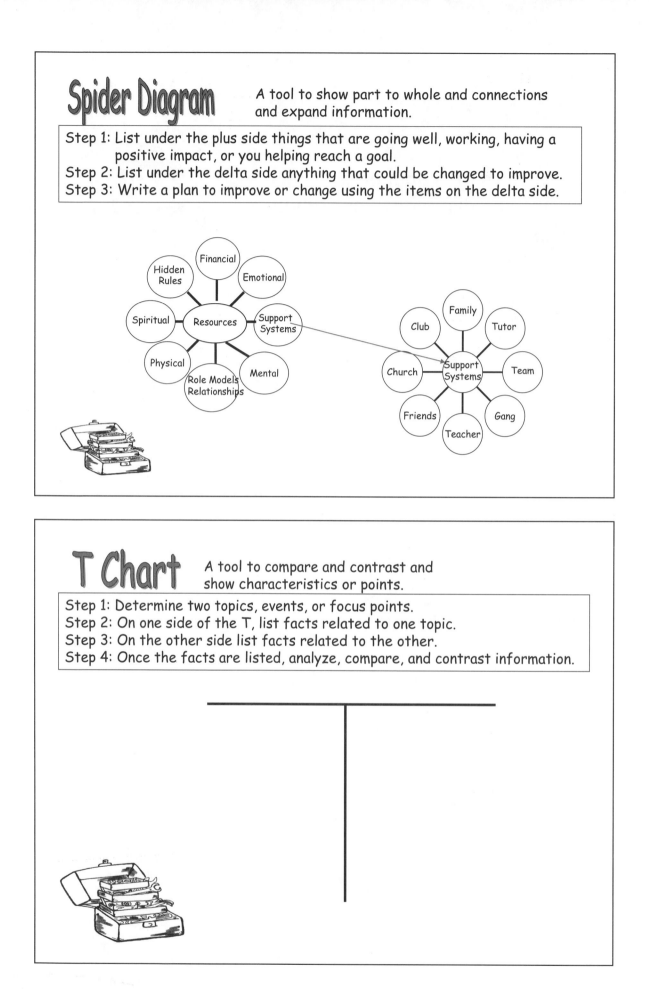

T Chart

A tool to compare and contrast and show characteristics or points.

Step 1: Determine two topics, events, or focus points.
Step 2: On one side of the T, list facts related to one topic.
Step 3: On the other side list facts related to the other.
Step 4: Once the facts are listed, analyze, compare, and contrast information.

Venn Diagram

A tool to show commonalities, sets, and subsets.

Step 1: Draw two circles as shown below. Determine two topics for comparison.
Step 2: In one circle list attributes, facts, or items related to one topic.
Step 3: In the other list traits, facts, or items related to the other topic.
Step 4: Any trait or fact that is shared by both is listed where circles overlap.

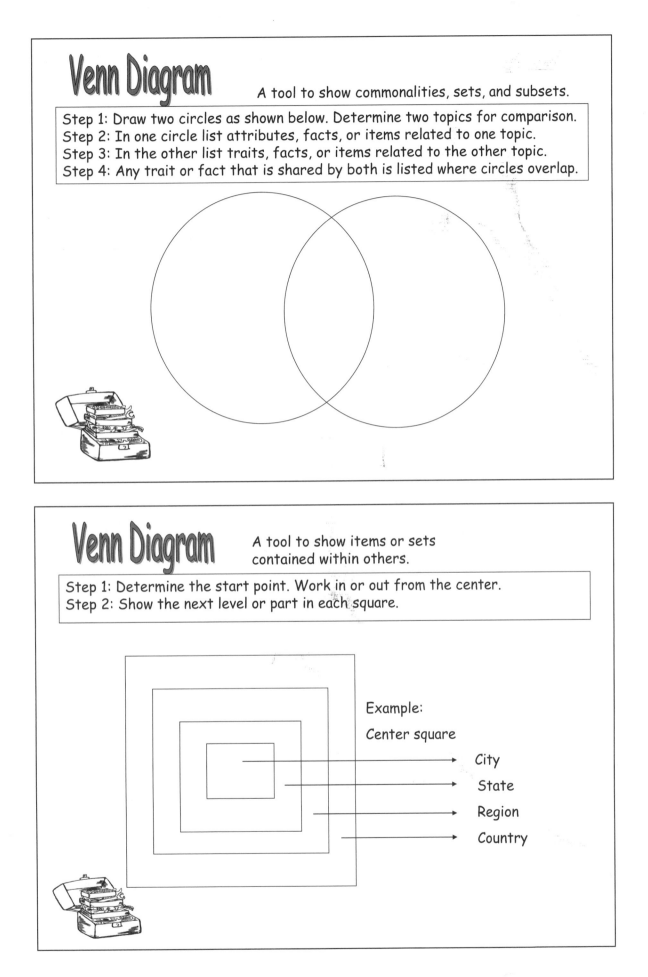

Venn Diagram

A tool to show items or sets contained within others.

Step 1: Determine the start point. Work in or out from the center.
Step 2: Show the next level or part in each square.

Example:

Center square

City

State

Region

Country

	Formal Definition	My Definition
	Mental Model	Relationships and Connections

Synonym: Antonym: Home Language:

Adapted from the work of Diane Paynter

Voice Bank Account
Chart deposits and withdrawals

	Child	Parent	Adult
Monday			
Tuesday			
Wednesday			
Thursday			
Friday			
Saturday			
Sunday			
Total			

21
days to change a habit

Deposits	Withdrawals

WWH

A tool for sorting and using information and identifying relationships and patterns.

Step 1: **What** Points out the *stimulus:* information, topic, or focus.
Step 2: **Why** States why the information is or is not important or relevant. *Explains* the meaning, consequences, or relationship.
Step 3: **How** Provides a strategy to answer the first two questions. How can or will the answers to the *what* and *why* be used?

What	Why	How

The Word, Term, or Concept	
Textbook, Teacher, Standard Definition	In my words
Formal register	Any register
Meets class requirements	My own words
Teacher or textbook words	Stated so I understand
Words that would appear on a test	
Mental Model	Connections, Purpose, or Pattern
Sketch or drawing	Shows relationships
Picture	Connections to other classes, subject areas, or systems
Story	Connections to experiences
Analogy or metaphor	Shows patterns or affinity
Pattern	Metaphor
Structure	Analogy
Purpose	
Synonym:	Antonym:	Home Language:

R Rule Definitions

Learn a word:

Consider the new word and what you know about it.

Write the definition in formal register.

Write your own definition in your own words.

Sketch the word or use a picture of the word.

Add information to create a mental model.

List connections to other subjects, knowledge.

Write synonyms and antonyms.

Write the word in home language.

Keep a vocabulary notebook: school and work

Abstract: the structures, labels, and mental models we use to represent the external reality in which we live. *Abstract* is the term for the representations used to translate concrete and sensory data into a form that can be stored in the mind. Abstract representations are mental models, pictures, words, and language. Abstract representational systems allow us to reframe information from sensory data and give values common understanding.

Action Plan (SMART): Strategy, Measurement, Action, Responsible/Resources, Timeline
Tells who will do what, when, and what strategies will be used.
A written plan to reach a goal listing the strategy or strategies and the steps and times to complete each.

What strategy will be used	Measurement	Action	Responsible Resources	Timeline
Practicing free throws to improve number made	Make 45 out of 50 shots daily Start: 20/50	50 shots every day	Me, basketball, court, shoes	September to January
Increase Stamina				

Aha!: the moment an individual is able to see the entire picture, the new picture, or reframe an old picture. The further the new picture is from the old one, the greater the aha! Paradigm shifts are aha! moments.

Analogy: a likeness or correspondence between one thing and another. Analogies are mental models because they teach the pattern, purpose, or structure, e.g., good guy: + + + + + +
In math a square number is a square number because it physically forms a square.
See Reframe.

$$9 = \begin{array}{c} XXX \\ XXX \\ XXX \end{array}$$

Assumptions: information or beliefs people use without proof that they are true.

Automaticity: the ability to act or complete a task automatically. To respond using previously learned skills or training without consciously focusing on the task.

Beliefs: an individual's realities, or what is perceived and accepted to be true or right.

Capital: assets such as money, property, networks, and other resources that represent the wealth of an individual, community, or business. There are many different types, including social, intellectual, physical, etc.
  Social capital: networks of relationships and connections with individuals and community that provide support. Examples: friends, relatives, business associates, members of clubs and organizations. Clubs, service organizations, businesses, agencies, and religious organizations comprise the social capital of a community. Bonding capital and bridging capital are two kinds of social capital. *Bonding capital* is the term for resources shared with those who have many of our same interests and connections—a family, team, etc. *Bridging capital* is the term for networks outside our normal circle. *Intellectual capital* is the term

for intangible assets or products generated using the mind or collective intelligence, e.g. information, creativity, knowledge, know-how, and expertise.

Career: the progression over time of an individual's work in a field or particular occupation he or she has been trained for. A career is a lifelong process unique to each person; careers include a sequence of work and development such as training, school, or participation in various jobs related to the field.

Case study: actual cases and examples studied in order to gather information and see patterns.

Cause and effect: the pattern showing an action and what happened in response to the action. Cause: You smile at someone. Effect: The person smiles back (or not). Use an If/Then tool to see cause and effect, patterns, and to predict and plan.

Child: anyone 18 years of age or younger.

Cognitive strategies: the strategies used to learn or learn about how you learn and think; fundamental ways of processing information. What, Why, and How is a strategy to improve learning processes and skills.

Comfort zone: the feeling individuals have when they are in a place where they feel physically or emotionally safe, know how to act, and will not be embarrassed or lose respect because of inappropriate actions or emotions.

Common language: the accepted and agreed-upon terms and language used by a group for shared or common understanding. See Relevance.

Concrete: a term for information or data that can actually be gathered using the five senses—sight, sound, touch, taste, smell; something actual or real.

Consequence: the effect; what happens when structure is not honored.

Continuum: a gradual transition from one situation or condition to another without a sudden break.

Coping strategies: all the ways individuals cope with daily living, disappointments, tragedies, and triumphs. They are ways of thinking about things, attitudes, self-talk, and strategies to resolve conflict and problems. They include goal setting, humor, and resources for resiliency.

Cue: verbal or nonverbal information that triggers a learned behavior. All groups of people use nonverbal cues and cueing mechanisms. *THE LOOK!*

Cueing mechanisms: the unwritten, often unspoken (nonverbal) cues we give one another.

Culture: the set of rules that governs the behaviors of certain groups; the values, beliefs, and expectations shared by most of a group's members.

Declarative knowledge: knowledge of facts, concepts, labels, and generalizations.

Dependent: dependence on others, unable to care for self without assistance. Lacking resources that allow one to be self-sufficient.

Discourse pattern:

Discourse Patterns:

FORMAL

CASUAL

Casual for gossip
Formal for a job interview

Let's get down to business

Let's visit

Fun Money

Disposable income: the amount of money that is available to spend on nonessentials. Money that is left after all of the bills are paid and other commitments are met.

Diversity: differences, or a group made up of individuals or things with different characteristics, talents, and/or beliefs.

Driving forces: the forces, criteria, information, beliefs, and events that drive actions or cause things to happen. The filter used to sort decisions and actions.

Economic class: term used for classification based on economic realities, resources, and individual choices about how to use them. Poverty, middle class, and wealth are the classifications used in this book.

Economic reality: the true state of resources, including money, available to an individual, or the truth about finances an individual must deal with every day. An example: It is a reality that an individual without a checking account may have to pay a fee to cash a paycheck at the bank.

Elephant in the room: phrase used to describe a problem that has a large impact on a situation but is being ignored or is not called by its actual name. Example: saying someone is asleep when they are actually passed out due to intoxication.

Emotional bank account: an analogy for relationships and the ability to develop and use emotional assets by making deposits and withdrawals.

a	bank account		a relationship account
like	money	is to	trust, friendship, and honor

Emotional memory bank: the database in the mind that stores experiences and the emotions attached to them. The memory bank is accessed to sort out feelings and appropriate behaviors. The small part of the mind, sometimes a little voice, that lets us know things feel right or that we should rethink a situation. Sometimes individuals will respond emotionally to a situation or event for no obvious reason. When this happens the individual must sort the feeling and the event to determine if the emotion is tied to the current event or has a connection to a past situation.

Expectations: the norms and expected behaviors of a group. What is expected to happen or is envisioned. Expectations may or may not be based on reality.

Force Field: tool to see driving forces and restraining forces.

Future picture: the vision or mental image of what the future will look like or is hoped to look like. A picture of a goal or future outcome that is used as a mental model for sorting and planning.

Generation: the act of creating something. Also the stages of descendents in a family: a grandfather, son, his son, etc. each represent a different generation.

Generational: a situation that has lasted two generations or longer. There are different patterns of behavior and mindsets when individuals have been in *any* economic class for two generations or longer.

Genre: kind, sort, style, or classification based on characteristics or composition. Mystery, romance, and fantasy are examples of genres of books.

Goal: what an individual wants to do, be, or have. SMART goals are Specific, Measurable, are Action-oriented, state Results, and have a Timeline. See Roadwork.

Habits: actions that are done automatically, unconsciously.

Hidden rules: the unspoken and unwritten cues and habits of a group. Refers to the patterns and unwritten and unspoken norms of a group.

If/Then: tool and strategy to see a pattern of cause and effect.

Learning process: a process that provides a way for people to see different realities, options, and beliefs and change habits of mind. This process can be used to change skills, understanding, and capabilities. *The R Rules* is a learning process.

Literacy: the state of being literate; able to use language to read, write, and speak. Various types of literacy are associated with different languages; e.g., street, boardroom, technological, etc.

Lotus Diagram: see Tools section. Used to sort, expand options, and show parts of a whole.

Mental model: a way to translate concrete or sensory information into abstract information so the mind can hold it. Mental models are the ways people think things or events should be and are used to sort, explain, and tell the structure, pattern, or purpose. Mental models are held in the mind in a variety of forms, including stories, analogies, and two-dimensional drawings.

Mentor: an individual who helps another learn and succeed. A mentor may be an individual who simply shows or guides you. A mentor may also be an individual who takes an interest in you and commits to helping you succeed.

Metacognition: the ability to think about your own thinking and the way you learn.

Mission statement: a statement of purpose. Tells why a group exists and what it will do.

Mutual respect: an environment in which structure, consequences, and choices exist.

Noblesse oblige: French term for the obligation of the noble or rich to use their wealth to help others who are less wealthy.

Norms: the behaviors, rules, or beliefs that are considered acceptable or normal by a given group.

Paradigm: how an individual views the world, he filter used to sort information and make decisions. Is the glass half-full or half-empty?

Paradigm shift: a change in the way an individual views the world or believes things to be.

an aha! moment

Patterns: a pattern is a model, plan, or design; a consistent style or behavior. Patterns occur when an event, behavior, or model is repeated; sets that occur over and over again. Patterns can be found in nature, people, behaviors, and cultures.

Plus Delta: +   Δ
tool for showing what is working (plus) and what might be changed (delta).

Predatory practices: practices or behaviors developed to gain an advantage based on others' lack of resources. Predators prey on others.

Process: a procedure or set of steps that occurs over time and generally produces an outcome. A process can be defined, repeated, and has a predictable outcome.

Race: a term for common bloodlines or descent. This is a lifelong resource that does not change.

Reactive: response based on outside influences; reacting generally based on emotions, feelings, or circumstances.

Reality: the actual current state of affairs *or* how the current state of affairs is believed to be. Realities can be real, perceptions, or beliefs. Realities are the set of facts that an individual must deal with.

Reason: the cause, driving force, reality, answer, or logic. See Reasons.

Reflection: looking into information or events and viewing what really happened and how it connects to your current situation. Generally requires time to think, sort, and use information.

Reframe: translate into a different form, as in concrete to abstract or casual to formal.

Registers of language: according to Dutch linguist Martin Joos, five registers are found in every language. School and work use formal register.

> Frozen: Pledge of Allegiance
> Formal: Textbooks
> Consultative: Classroom
> Casual: Friends
> Intimate: Twins, lovers, language of sexual harassment

5

Relationship: the connections, patterns, and interactions between people or things. In any relationship there are usually an agreed-upon set of behaviors, rules, roles, and structures. Relationships are connections and patterns. Each relationship is as unique as the individuals, the subjects, or things that are involved, and the time and place in which the interaction occurs.

Relationship of mutual respect: a relationship between individuals where differences and likenesses are accepted, celebrated, and used for mutual benefit.

Relative: based on comparison, related to or in relationship to.

Representation: anything used to represent another thing; a sketch, story, symbol, mental model, etc.

Resiliency: the capacity to spring back, rebound, successfully adapt in the face of adversity, and develop social competence despite exposure to extreme stress.

Resources: anything available to a person that can be used to support or help, especially in a difficult situation. Eight resources covered here: financial, emotional, mental, spiritual, physical, support systems, relationships and role models, and knowledge of hidden rules. Each of these resources plays a vital role in the success of an individual. Also: assets or capital. See Resources.   *Resources = Choices*

Respect: a judgment based on actions that is earned, taught, and given between individuals.

Response: any reaction to a stimulus; the "effect" in "cause and effect."

Restraining force: forces or barriers that hold one back; see *Force Field*.

Rigor: unwavering standards, structure, or expectations, as in academic content standards; the requirements to pass a class, graduate, get a certificate, etc. Essential facts and learning needed to succeed in a class, course, or job.

Role of an educator: "The role of the educator or social worker is to offer a support system, role models, and opportunities to learn that will increase the likelihood of the person's success. Ultimately, the choice always belongs to the individual."   –Dr. Ruby Payne

Role model: a person you use as a model to pattern actions after. A person who provides a picture of what you do or don't want to be, do, or have.

Root cause: a term for the real reason or the base of the problem. Like tree roots, the root cause is what supports or feeds a cause.

Scenario: a brief overview of a situation and events with limited details; used to plan or predict; stories, cases, or situations.

Scripts: the program; the written set of actions that will be followed.
Example: the set of actions followed in a computer program, play, movie, or television program.

Self-talk: the little voice inside our heads that talks to us all the time when we are thinking, learning, questioning, or completing a task.

> *Negative self-talk:* Negative self-talk is the little voice, usually a child or parent voice, that questions why we did or said something, blames, accuses, or uses words that cause or reinforce negative self-images.
>
> *Positive self-talk:* Positive self-talk is the little voice that gives us encouraging messages, lists steps and plans to help complete tasks, and provides support and direction to get through situations.
>
> *Procedural self-talk:* Procedural self-talk is the little voice that talks us through a task or process. It is learned and can be taught when growing up or developed at any age by using a process of mediation to ask what, why, and how.

Situational: due to a situation and generally thought of as temporary until the situation changes.
Situational poverty can be due to the loss of a job, a death, or a change in a situation that reduces resources.
Relative to resources, it is when a situation has caused a change. See *generational* to compare information.

SMART: acronym for Specific, Measurable, Action, Realistic (and Resources), and Timeline. Use when setting goals or developing an action plan.

Social class: classification based on social status and popularity. Social class is not entirely determined by economic classification.

Social cues: verbal or nonverbal cues or cueing mechanisms used by a group of individuals that indicate whether or not behavior is appropriate. Examples: THE LOOK! Also avoidance, or if an individual gets quiet or seems uncomfortable around another or the group.

Stamina: sticking to it when times are tough. Examples: courage, endurance, energy to stay.

Stereotype: a model or stamp used to classify an entire group without considering variation and patterns.

Stimulus: the action or event that generates a response; the cause in "cause and effect"

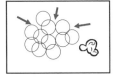

Story structure:

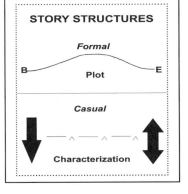

STORY STRUCTURES

Formal

B — Plot — E

Casual

^   ^   ^

Characterization

The structure and patterns used to tell a story. Formal register uses a beginning, middle, and end. Different genres use different patterns or story structures.

Support systems: any system that provides support; the system of family, friends, and backup resources that can be accessed in times of need. They are divided and listed in seven categories here:
(1) information and know-how; (2) procedural self-talk (3) goal setting; (4) coping strategies; (5) problem solving options; (6) relief; and (7) positive self-talk.

Positive support systems do not ask individuals to engage in destructive behavior.

Syntax: the proper order of a language. The order the words are arranged in; for example, adjectives coming before nouns. English syntax calls for "the pretty girl" instead of "the girl pretty."

Think out of the box: a phrase for thinking beyond normal or accepted limits or norms. Thinking out of the box is the ability to see possibilities and options beyond the limits of conventional thinking and norms.

Tools: mental models, drawings, and processes that can be used to sort and organize data. Tools create a picture of information or data and translate concrete into abstract. They allow discussions to focus on systems and issues rather than individuals.

Vision: something seen without using regular sight; a mental picture, a dream, mental model, or statement of what you want the future to look like.

Visualization: an activity to create a mental picture or vision in the mind.

Voice: inside everyone's head are three internal voices that guide the individual. They are the child voice, the parent voice, and the adult voice. These are the little voices that give messages, help finish tasks, complete projects, determine behaviors, and help negotiate choices. When an individual must act as an adult at an early age, the adult voice is not developed, nor is the ability to negotiate and communicate. Strategies can be used to develop the adult voice and increase resources. See Register.

What, Why, and How (WWH): a mediation or tool that is used to understand and learn about what things or actions are, why they occur or are important, and how individuals can use the information or respond. WWH is used in a learning process.

Work: any task an individual sets his or her hand, mind, and resources to accomplish. May be done for pay or as a volunteer, but should not be confused with a job where the employee receives a salary. *Work* in this sense is associated with purpose or cause.

Bibliography

"16 Career Clusters, The." (2008). States' Career Clusters Initiative. Accessed at http://www.careerclusters. org/16clusters.cfm, April 14.

Andrews, Andy. (2006). Keynote address at the New Mexico Public Education All Kids Conference. Hyatt Regency Tamaya. Bernalillo, NM, June 1.

Angelou, Maya. (2007). "A Conversation with Dr. Maya Angelou." Accessed at http://sites.target.com/site/en/corporate/page.jsp?contentId=PRD03-003811, May 20.

ASCA National Model: A Framework for School Counseling Programs. (2003). Alexandria, VA: American School Counselor Association.

ASCA National Model Workbook. (2004). Alexandria, VA: American School Counselor Association.

Bandler, Richard, and Grinder, John. (1979). *Frogs into Princes.* Moab, UT: Real People Press.

Breaking Ranks: Changing an American Institution. (1996). Reston, VA: National Association of Secondary School Principals.

Brown, Glenda. (1998). "Quality in the Classroom: Strengthening Quality in Schools." Energy Training Center, Kirtland Air Force Base. Albuquerque, NM, April 14 and 15.

Bruett, Karen. "Real and Relevant 21st Century Skills." *Converge* February 2006: 60–65.

Carroll, Lewis. (1889). *Alice's Adventures in Wonderland.* New York, NY: Macmillan.

Choices and Consequences. (1997). Ed Brazee and Ross Burkhardt, creators. New York: Courtroom Television Network.

Clark, Ron. (2003). *The Essential 55.* New York: Hyperion.

Comer, James. (2005). Keynote Address, Association for Supervision and Curriculum Development Conference. San Francisco Marriott. San Francisco, CA, October 24.

Covey, Sean. (1998). *The 7 Habits of Highly Effective Teens.* New York: Simon & Schuster.

Covey, Stephen. (1989). *The 7 Habits of Highly Effective People: Powerful Lessons In Personal Change.* New York: Simon & Schuster.

Covey, Stephen. (2004). *The 8th Habit: From Effectiveness to Greatness.* New York: Simon & Schuster.

Daggett, Willard. (2003). "Rigor and Relevance." Quality in Education Conference. Hyatt Regency. Albuquerque, NM, September 23.

Deming, W. Edwards. (1982). *Out of the Crisis.* Cambridge, MA: MIT Press.

DeVol, Philip. (2004). *Getting Ahead in a Just-Gettin'-By World: Building Your Resources for a Better Life.* Highlands, TX: aha! Process.

Drucker, Peter. (1992). *Managing for the Future: The 1990s and Beyond.* New York: Truman Talley.

Dusa, Gail. (2000). *Practical Activities for Achieving Success with Difficult and At-Risk Students.* Madison,WI: National At-Risk Education Network.

Eaker, Robert. (2006). Presentation to educators. 20th Street Conference Center. Farmington, NM, November 30.

Eaker, Robert, DuFour, Richard, and DuFour, Rebecca. (2002). *Getting Started: Reculturing Schools to Become Professional Learning Communities.* Bloomington, IN: National Educational Service.

Eaker, Robert, et al. (2004). *Whatever it Takes: How Professional Learning Communities Respond When Kids Don't Learn.* Bloomington, IN: Solution Tree.

East, Grant. (1997). "Rules Without Relationships Breed Rebellion." *Texas Study of Secondary Education* 6.2: 12–14, and 25.

Ellis, Kim D. (2007). *Cookin' in the Classroom!* Highlands, TX: aha! Process, Inc.

Exploring Opportunity: A High School Student's Guide to College. (2003). Santa Fe, NM: New Mexico Commission on Higher Education.

Farella, John. (1990). *The Main Stalk: A Synthesis of Navajo Philosophy.* Tucson, AZ: University of Arizona.

Feuerstein, Reuven, et al. (1980). *Instrumental Enrichment: An Intervention Program for Cognitive Modifiability*. Glenview, IL: Scott, Foresman & Co.

Frankl, Victor. (1959). *Man's Search for Meaning*. Boston, MA: Beacon Press.

Gandhi, Arun. (2000). "Reflections of Peace." *Brigham Young University Magazine* Spring. Accessed at http://magazine.byu.edu/?act=view&a=152, March 29.

Garrison, Webb. (1992). *Why You Say It*. Nashville, TN: Rutledge Hill.

Gladwell, Malcolm. (2005). *Blink: The Power of Thinking Without Thinking*. New York: Time Warner.

Goleman, Daniel. (1998). *Working with Emotional Intelligence*. New York: Bantam.

Gruwell, Erin. (1999). *The Freedom Writer's Diary*. New York: Broadway.

Hanson, Linda. (2003). *Poverty Project*. St. Paul, MN: Good Ground.

Hart, Betty, and Risley, Todd. (1999). *Meaningful Differences in the Everyday Experience of Young American Children*. Baltimore, MD: Brookes.

Henry, Annie, and Milstein, Mike. (2001). "Helping School Leaders Build Strong Relationships with Their Communities Using Resiliency Strategies." Presented to the New Mexico Coalition for School Administrators. Hyatt Regency Hotel. Albuquerque, NM, July 23.

Jackson, Tom. (1993). *Activities That Teach*. Telluride, CO: Red Rock.

Jalongo, Mary Renck. (1991). *Creating Learning Communities: The Role of the Teacher in the 21st Century*. Bloomington, IN: National Education Service.

Jenkins, Lee. (2004). *Permission to Forget: And Nine Other Root Causes of America's Frustration with Education*. Milwaukee, WI: ASQ Quality Press.

Jodi's Stories. (2006). Featuring Jodi Pfarr. DVD. Highlands, TX: aha! Process.

Joos, Martin. (1967). *The Five Clocks: A Linguistic Excursion into the Five Styles of English Usage*. New York: Harcourt, Brace, and World.

Kuhn, Thomas. (1962). *The Structure of Scientific Revolutions*. Chicago: University of Chicago.

Levitt, Stephen, and Dubner, Stephen. (2005). *Freakonomics*. New York: William Morrow.

Levine, Mel. (2002). *A Mind at a Time*. New York: Simon & Schuster.

Lucas, Timothy R. (2003). Presentation at Schools That Learn Conference. Marriott Manhattan. New York, July 1.

Macklin, J.W. Extemporaneous comments at *The 8th Habit* book release. Snowbird Resort. Park City, Utah, November 4.

March of the Penguins. (2005). Luc Jacquet, dir. Bonne Pioche.

Illustrated Treasury of Children's Literature. (1955). Margaret E. Martignoni, ed. New York: Grosset and Dunlap.

Marzano, Robert. (1992). *A Different Kind of Classroom: Teaching with Dimensions of Learning*. Alexandria, VA: Association for Supervision and Curriculum Development.

Marzano, Robert. (2003). *School Leadership That Works: From Research to Results*. Alexandria, VA: Association for Supervision and Curriculum Development.

Marzano, Robert. (2003). *What Works in Schools: Translating Research into Action*. Alexandria, VA: Association for Supervision and Curriculum Development.

Marzano, Robert. (2004). *Building Background Knowledge for Academic Achievement*. Alexandria, VA: Association for Supervision and Curriculum Development.

Marzano, Robert, et al. (2001). *A Handbook for Classroom Instruction*. Alexandria, VA: Association for Supervision and Curriculum Development.

Marzano, Robert, Pickering, Debra, and Pollock, Jane. (2001). *Classroom Instruction That Works: Research- Based Strategies for Increasing Student Achievement*. Alexandria, VA: Association for Supervision and Curriculum Development.

Marzano, Robert, and Pickering, Debra. (2005). *Building Academic Vocabulary: Teacher's Manual*. Alexandria, VA: Association for Supervision and Curriculum Development.

McClanahan, Elaine, and Wicks, Carolyn. (1993). *Future Force: Kids That Want To, Can, and Do!* Chino Hills, CA: PACT Publishing.

Merriam-Webster's Encyclopedia of Literature. (1995). Kathleen Kuiper, ed. Springfield, MA: Merriam and Webster.

Miller, Scott C. (2008). *Until It's Gone: Ending Poverty in Our Nation, in Our Lifetime.* Highlands, TX: aha! Process.

Mitchell, W. (2002). Video Presentation: *It's Not What Happens To You, It's What You Do About It.* Arvada, CO: W Mitchell.

Montano-Harmon, Maria Rosario. (1991). "Discourse Features of Written Mexican Spanish: Current Research in Contrastive Rhetoric and Its Implications. *Hispania* 74.2: 417–425.

Morrison, Toni. (1999). *The Big Box.* New York: Hyperion.

National Career Development Guidelines (NCDG). (1994, 2004). Washington, D.C.: U.S. Department of Education Office of Vocational and Adult Education.

O'Banion, Terry. (1997). *A Learning College for the 21st Century.* Phoenix, AZ: American Council on Education/Oryx Press.

O'Neil, John. (1995). "On Schools As Learning Organizations: A Conversation with Peter Senge." *Educational Leadership* 52.7: 20-23.

"Oprah's Debt Diet." (2008). Oprah.com. Accessed at http://www.oprah.com/money/debtdiet/money_debtdiet_main.jhtml, April 14.

Patterson, Kerry, et al. (2002). *Crucial Conversations: Tools for Talking When Stakes Are High.* New York: McGraw Hill.

Payne, Ruby. (1999). *Preventing School Violence by Creating Emotional Safety.* Highlands, TX: aha! Process.

Payne, Ruby. (2002). *Understanding Learning: The How, the Why, and the What.* Highlands, TX: aha! Process.

Payne, Ruby. (2005). *A Framework for Understanding Poverty,* (4th Revised Edition). Highlands, TX: aha! Process.

Payne, Ruby. (2005). *Crossing the Tracks for Love.* Highlands, TX: aha! Process.

Payne, Ruby. (2005). *Learning Structures* (3rd Revised Edition). Highlands, TX: aha! Process.

Payne, Ruby, DeVol, Philip, and Smith, Terie Druessi. (2001). *Bridges Out of Poverty.* Highlands, TX: aha! Process.

Payne, Ruby, and Krabill, Don. (2002). *Hidden Rules of Class at Work.* Highlands, TX: aha! Process.

Payne, Ruby, and Magee, Donna. (2001). *Meeting Standards and Raising Test Scores: When You Don't Have Much Time or Money,* (Revised Edition). Highlands, TX: aha! Process.

Paynter, Diane. (2005–2008). *Strengthening Vocabulary.* Multiple presentations. Farmington Municipal School District, Farmington, NM.

Paynter, Diane, Bodrova, Elena, and Doty, Jane. (2005). *For the Love of Words.* San Francisco, CA: Jossey-Bass.

People Like Us: Social Class In America. (2001). Louis Alvarez and Andrew Kolker, dirs. DVD. WETA and Center for New American Media.

Peregoy, Janet. (2002). Presentation at Quality New Mexico Conference. Old Town Sheraton. Albuquerque, NM, March 8.

Prize Winner of Defiance, Ohio, The. (2005). Jane Anderson, dir. DreamWorks.

Rita's Stories. (2003). Featuring Rita Pierson. DVD. Highlands, TX: aha! Process, Inc.

Reeves, Douglas. (2002). *The Daily Disciplines of Leadership.* San Francisco, CA: Jossey-Bass.

Ron Clark Story, The. (2006). Randa Haines, dir. TV movie. The Alberta Film Development Program of the Alberta Foundation for the Arts.

Rudy. (1993). David Anspaugh, dir. DVD. TriStar Pictures.

Sroka, Stephen R. (2005). "Making a Difference with the Power of One: The Double Crib." Keynote address, Association for Supervision and Curriclum Development Conference. San Francisco Marriott. San Francisco, CA, October 24.

Saxe, John Godfrey. (1878). "The Blind Men and the Elephant." *Poetry of America*. W.J. Litton, ed. New York: George Bell and Sons.

Schargel, Franklin. (2003). *Dropout Prevention Tools*. Larchmont, NY: Eye on Education.

Schargel, Franklin, and Smink, Jay. (2001). *Strategies to Help Solve Our School Dropout Problem*. Larchmont, NY: Eye On Education.

Schumacher, Marie. (2006). Presentation on Career Clusters. San Juan College. Farmington, NM, April 4.

Senge, Peter, et al. (2000). *Schools That Learn: A Fifth Discipline Fieldbook for Educators, Parents, and Everyone Who Cares About Education*. New York: Doubleday.

Senge, Peter, et al. (1994). *The Fifth Discipline Fieldbook*. New York: Doubleday.

Slocumb, Paul. (2004). *Hear Our Cry: Boys in Crisis*. Highlands, TX: aha! Process.

Smith, Betty. (1943). *A Tree Grows In Brooklyn*. New York: Harper.

Stay in the Groove. (2002). Santa Fe, NM: New Mexico Department of Labor.

Stailey, Jay, and Payne, Ruby. (1998). *Think Rather of Zebra: Dealing with Aspects of Poverty Through Story*. Highlands, TX: aha! Process.

Stafford, William. (1993). "A Ritual to Read to Each Other." *The Darkness Around Us Is Deep: Selected Poems of William Stafford*. Robert Bly, ed. New York: Harper Perennial.

Tomlinson, Carol Ann. (1999). *The Differentiated Classroom: Responding to the Needs of All Learners*. Alexandria, VA: Association for Supervision and Curriculum Development.

Tough Choices Tough Times: The Report of the New Commission on the Skills of the American Workforce. (2007). Washington, D.C.: National Center on Education and the Economy.

Tucker, Bethanie. (2005). *The Journey of Al and Gebra to the Land of Algebra*. Highlands, TX: aha! Process.

Wade, Carole, and Tavris, Carol. (1999). *Invitation to Psychology*. Upper Saddle River, NY: Prentice Hall.

"Wage Information for Job Seekers: Northern WIA Area." (2007). Santa Fe, NM: New Mexico Department of Labor, Economic Research and Analysis Bureau.

What Work Requires of Schools: A SCANS Report for America. (2000). Prepared by The Secretary's Commission on Achieving Necessary Skills. Washington, D.C.: United States Department of Labor.

Wheatley, Margaret. (1994). *Leadership and the New Science: Learning about Organization from an Orderly Universe*. San Francisco: Berrett-Koehler.

Wicks, Carolyn, Peregoy, Janet, and Wheeler, Jo. (2001). *Plugged In!* New Bern, NC: Class Action.

Williamson, Marianne. (1992). *A Return to Love: Reflections on the Principles of a Course in Miracles*. New York: HarperCollins.

Your Job Will You Keep it Or Lose It? (2001). Santa Fe, NM: New Mexico Department of Labor.